Thai Hawker Food

Publisher	Clive Wing
Editorial Coordination	Book Promotion & Service Ltd.
Text by	Kenny Yee
	Catherine Gordon
Illustrated by	Sun Win
Marketing & Sales	*International Sales & Foreign Rights:*

Book Promotion & Service Ltd.
2220/31 Soi Ramkhamhaeng 36/1
Huamark Bangkok 10240 THAILAND
Tel: (02) 375-2685-6, 732-0243-5, 732-1954-8
Fax: (02) 375-2669
Email : info@book.co.th
http ://www.book.co.th

First Edition 1993

Copyright © 2001, 1996, 1993 by Book Promotion & Service Ltd.

ISBN : 974-89009-9-1

In preparing this book

A field survey was undertaken by a couple of university students, in addition to other back-ups, interviews and researches by others. Just before printing, our marketing team did a double check of sites, sketches, snapshots and facts.

The information is thus as fresh as a cucumber.

Though hawkers move, chances are the same ones will be there for some time to come since most lay a 'territorial claim' to a particular site.

Many move only from home to 'office'.

Have a delicious time!

CONTENTS

WHERE YOU CAN FIND...   *PAGE*

FOREWORD   8

IDENTIFYING THE HAWKER   11

GROUPING THE FOOD   12
   Main Dishes. Noodles. Snacks. Desserts.
   Beverages.

THE BASIC CONDIMENTS   13

TELL - TALE UTENSILS & INGREDIENTS   14
   Electric rice cooker. Shimmering deep pan.
   Bubbling enamel basin. Mortar and pestle.
   Frying pan. The wok; flat-bottomed type.
   Aluminium pot. Wicker basket,
   with curled up noodles. Steamboat.
   Claypot. Goldfish bowl.

PREPARATION STYLES   18

TIPS TO THE TABLE   23
> Where to sit. *Aroy mai*?

'STUCK - UP' HAWKERS   25
> 'Stone-deaf zombies.' Shallow-memory
> 'waiters.'

TAKE- AWAY PACKET   26
> Different ways of the same thing.

THE EXPERIENCE IS IN THE EATING   28
> The hygiene question.

THE FOOD   29
> Each item individually described.
> In glass show-cases.   29
> Over the charcoal.   38
> Slow steamed-done.   44
> Quick fried.   50
> Deep-oil fried.   53
> Ready-cooked food.   57
> Ice-cool way.   62
> Keeping it warm.   66
> Special category.   68

HEADING TO THE AREAS 74

Around the City of Angels. All these
areas are marked on the map of Bangkok.

1. **Silom**... the 'Wall Street' of Bangkok.   76
2. **Pratunam**... popular 'shopping square.'   78
3. **Banglumpoo** ... 'budget travellers' haunt.   80
4. **Chatuchak**...biggest open-air
   weekend market.   82
5. **Soi Tonglo**..a high-class residential area.   84
6. **Siam Square**...
   around three movie halls.   85
7. **Bangrak**...just off Silom/Surawong Roads.   86
8. **Chinatown**... Sam Peng/Yaowarat,
   very noisy places.   87
9. **Soi Nana Nua thru' Soi Cowboy**...
   tourist walking street.   89
10. **Klong Toey**... where its renowned wet
   market is.   91
11. **Transport Terminals**;   92
     11.1: Hualumpong...
      Central Railway Station.   92
     11.2: Morchit...
       North/Northeastern Terminal.   93
     11.3: Ekamai...Eastern Seaboard Terminal.   93
     11.4: Sai Tai Mai...Southern Bus Terminal.   93

12. 'Non-Tourist Areas'

    12.1: **Saphan Kwai**... near Chatuchak Market.   **94**

    12.3: **Ramkhamhaeng** ...

            near the campus.   **95**

    12.3: **Tha Prajan**, near the Grand Palace.   **96**

    12.4: **Theves**   **97**

    12.5: **Victory Monument**   **98**

    12.6: **Thonburi**   **99**

    12.7: **Phrakhanong**...Soi 71 Sukhumvit Road,

            magnet of factory workers.   **100**

MAP OF BANGKOK   **102**

    Locating the hawker sites

SAY IT IN THAI   **104**

    How to blabber useful terms, phrases.

WHAT THE DOCTOR SAYS   **109**

    (and grandma added).

THE HAWKER OF YESTERDAY   **112**

    A brief look back.

TO YOU, ESPECIALLY   **115**

    Share something with us?

WRAPPING FOOD THAI STYLE   **117**

FOREWORD

Why this book?

Because one of the best ways to know the Land of Smiles is to eat and to enjoy eating the way locals typically do.

Do many people eat hawker food?

Urban-planning lecturer Khwansuang Atibodhi of Chulalongkorn University said at a 'City Life' seminar in 1991:

> *"Actually, roadside food vendors are also an important part of city life. They help millions of people each day to fill their stomachs at cheap prices."*

The aim of this book is to help the reader identify a particular hawker food regardless of where it is being sold. It is not to single out and claim that one particular stall is better than another since this is a matter of personal taste. We leave it to the reader to discover and discern.

One warning: most Thai food is pungent and spicy so go easy on the very first spoonful. It can be hot in both senses. By the same token, this makes the food extra special.

Thailand is a paradise for hawker food and this book is probably the first complete easy-to-know and easy-to-find list of nearly all available dishes one is likely to encounter. Each item is described in detail.

Sketches show where stalls are concentrated; a glossary provides some guidelines to the local language and for added reading pleasure we have included some medical tips and grandma's myths.

Most helpful of all, we think, is that we have also put the Thai script next to the English equivalent for each food item. The reason for doing this needs no explanation: just point out the item and give your widest blank smile to the hawker if all else fails.

These 'moving restaurants' are a challenge to locals too, in the multitudes of dishes offered and the expanse of hawking territory.

Your 'dining hall' may just be a small table with uneven legs and seasoned chairs crammed onto the smallest section of an already crowded narrow walkway. Or you are your own eating hall: standing up, leaning against a doorway, sitting in a park chair or resting on the stairs of a modern building. No problem, *mai pen rai*, as the Thai loves to say; feel free, feel at home; enjoy life, enjoy hawker food. Try everything once.

If you hold your chopsticks left-handed and sit too close to a right-handed glutton, you may be engaged in a hand-to-hand combat!

Prepared to do battle?
Then, turn the pages!

IDENTIFYING THE HAWKER

The humble hawker is a traditional and characteristic figure all over Thailand, offering home-made specialities at prices below those in air-conditioned dining halls and major restaurants.

The hawker may be stationary during the course of his serving hours or he may ramble along, pushing his cart or shouldering his baskets of paraphernalia. He may also be hawking his wares in a sole basket rested on a shoulder; or he may look as if he is moving house, with what looks like a collection of all his household effects with his children walking alongside protectively.

The easiest way to spot a hawker is to look for the seller's mobility: wheels fixed to a cart or the couple of baskets sandwiching him. In this context, similar-looking stalls placed in front of eating shops are not considered 'hawkers' for our purposes, though quite often the nature of food sold is the same. (One could thus opt to order from an eating shop instead.)

An exception to this mode of identification is the popular Chatuchak Weekend Market where hawkers are sited at fixed rental bays, as are those seen in 'wet' markets. Otherwise, hawkers are easily found at street junctions on the walkways, around places of entertainment, along *sois* or lanes and practically everywhere else where there is space and crowd, like around office blocks, department stores, leisure parks and even in hospital grounds. Put another way, for the enthusiastic visitor, Thailand is a Hawkers' Paradise.

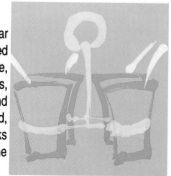

GROUPING THE FOOD

Probably the biggest headache for first-timers is to figure out just what is being sold. A few pointers for some background 'homework' might help to eliminate confusion.

In all cases, there are tell-tale 'trade marks' and once they are spotted, the rest is easy; but first note that being hawkers, each one concentrates on only one major 'category' of food. These categories can be grouped broadly, for eating purposes, under five headings:

❖ *main dishes or full meal type*. This would be rice with separately prepared dishes that come in individual small plates or, as with most local meals, everything comes lumped on top of the rice on a single plate.

❖ *noodles of all sizes*. Noodles, invented and introduced in Thailand by the Chinese, are taken as a main lunch or dinner by everyone.

❖ *snacks*, of all sorts. As this book covers the most popular items, there are many tidbits and sweets that you would almost certainly discover.

❖ *desserts*. There are many specialities and even more when seasonal fruits abound, like mango which is taken with glutinous rice. Weight watchers will be pleased to know that most local desserts and sweets are not as fattening as say, an apple pie or a creamy chocolate cake.

❖ *beverages*. Some are considered cooling for the body system while others are recommended for health. Most of course are simply thirst quenchers or liquid refreshments for the sunny climate.

Chopsticks and a soup spoon are the customary cutlery weapons for food fighting, but fork and spoon will accompany rice meals. Should chopsticks be unmanageable ask for a fork and spoon but be prepared to be greeted only with an apologetic smile.

THE BASIC CONDIMENTS

Condiments are as much a part of the meal as is the food itself. Many foreigners miss out on this. Taken without condiments the food feels tasteless to the local tongue. If these toppings - soy sauce, dry chilli flakes, cut chillies in vinegar, sugar and sometimes ground peanuts - are not already on the table, the server will hunt these out for you.

Condiments come in separate containers that are slotted into a carrying tray. You select and sprinkle. You have to move fast for the whole basket may be whisked away to another customer.

It is hard to find any Thai eating a meal without first bombarding the food with ingredients. In fact, the soup will be so adulterated that it will often take on a new brownish red colouring.

The best idea is to sprinkle each condiment bit by bit or, for the more adventurous, try everything at once and take it from there. Note that pepper and salt do not constitute a-la-carte street food eating in Thailand. It is almost an impossibility to ask for them as one does in the West. Where you do see a pepper shaker on the table, the hawker is ninety-nine percent Chinese-Thai and the food is ninety-nine percent rice porridge (congee).

TELL-TALE UTENSILS AND INGREDIENTS

❖ **Specialised utensils** probably explain best what a hawker is up to, so here are some of the most popular types of hawkers' 'trade marks'. Pick up these few points and the road to the stomach should be easier.

Electric rice cooker
Obviously, cooked plain white rice is the mainstay. This means maybe no noodles, if no noodles are seen. Next thing is to see if there are containers looking like oblong surgical trays with already-cooked dishes on a make-shift table. Or steamed whole chicken hooked up alongside red-crusted crispy pork flanks in a glass showcase.

You would have already guessed these two types of food by now. See how easy it is? Of course it is rice with ready-cooked dishes or chicken rice (and/or also, red roast-pork rice or duck rice, if only ducks are in the showcase). In many cases, if ducks are seen, only duck rice is sold; in others, a mix is available.

A brass pan/basin, simmering on a stove somewhere nearby. The pan would have a pair of ears. Brownish meat slices would be bubbling like a volcano about to erupt, steam floating up. This is beef-only soup: meat pieces, meat balls and in the simmering pot, the insides and tendons. Very delicious to locals but very eye opening - and sometimes mouth as well - to foreigners.

A big enamel basin with pig's legs simmering in thick brown sauce. Try to spot some plain-boiled vegetables. This is stewed pork legs. Also available usually is red-roast pork rice.

A dark brown burnt-clay mortar with a wooden pestle.
Note its slender bottom shape, which is different from a kitchen-only granite pounder. The main dish here is papaya salad *som tam*, an invasion from the Northeast *I-saan* Provinces. A few other preparations are available and hawkers all sell the same items. These are *larb*, *nam tok* and sometimes *tom krueng nai*. Also there may be chicken being deep-fried or grilled in front of your eyes.

Locals, particularly Northeastern workers could be seen at tables where local whisky and soda make up the general evening get-together.

Frying pan, over a charcoal/gas stove.
This utensil, (the 'Chinese wok' in European countries) is a 'must' in Thai or Asian homes and its versatility is amazing. A frying pan means you can order a good variety of food: fried rice, fried noodles, 'a-la-carte'combination depending on what ingredients the hawker has.

The **wok** is also used in deep-frying of snacks like bananas or yam; chicken legs, breasts, wings, feet, necks; locusts, birds; many kinds of meat balls and flour cakes of all sorts.

The **flat** frying pan is popular for roti, stuffed vegetable puddings and various types of cake-like stuffings.

Rows of aluminium pots would mean two things: ready-cooked food or prepared desserts usually to go with crushed ice.

To discover what is inside the pots, some wrist exercise is needed. The cooked dishes would be the accompaniments for white (i.e. not fried) rice. A king-size pot or tub with a conical cover is steamed herbal-meat soup served in individual Chinese porcelain bowls.

These pots are gradually being replaced by neatly arranged trays with hot water underneath in an all-encompassing cabinet. Sometimes but not usually, these trays have covers as well. This 'style' is found more in proper eating shops than with hawkers in the open air.

Two huge enamel pots with curry fish balls. Nearby would be a wicker basket with twirled-up white noodles while a long table with plates of vegetables suggest the toppings.

This is very common and it is 'Thai Noodles with Fish Curry Sauce' *Khanom-jeen Narm Ya*. This is the only food where you can eat as much as you can of the raw vegetables for no extra charge. And *khanom-jeen* is easily the queen of the cheapest of the cheap food.

Glass showcases. This is by far the most common hawker food-storing cabinet and many entirely different kinds of meals can be cooked from the 'ammunition' kept in the glass cases.

First, rice meals. If you can see uncut tomato, whole cucumber and eggs in one corner and raw meat pieces (pork, beef and chicken) in bowls or plates in another, you may order fried rice.

Then there is rice in watery form - congee or porridge *joak*. Here, look also for a small pot with a handle for boiling the *joak*. This dish is on the street either as an early breakfast or a late evening snack. It's hard to find it for lunch.

Of the rice-based meals, look in the showcases for hanging poultry and order chicken rice, or duck rice, or roast pork rice accordingly.

Next is noodles. Here, two distinct categories can be discerned. One is strictly yellow-egg-noodles *bah mee* and the other is a variety of white rice noodles in different thicknesses. The widest and flattest is *sen yai*; the smaller and flat one is *sen lek*, the thinnest is *sen mee*, and the yellow egg noodles *bah mee*. A fifth category is *woon sen* (bean vermicelli), a very thin, slippery and transparent noodle.

In popular tourist areas like Silom and Chatuchak, macaroni can be ordered, especially at stalls selling noodles as well.

The glass case may also house oysters for frying, cuttle fish, morning glory vegetables for *yen tao fo* and other Asian quick food. Look and try to determine; herein lies the challenge. Don't just see and go away.

Steamboat. In Thailand, two kinds of food make use of this receptacle. One is *suki* and the other is the all-famous *tom yum*. Both preparations may come without this water/soup heater though if not specifically requested.

The steamboat is a boiling pot with a charcoal compartment in the centre. A lazier modern version uses gas/electricity instead of coal. It has a funnel not unlike that of a steamship, hence its name.

Claypot is for slow cooking over a fire. Anything cooked in a claypot takes longer to be ready and thus costs slightly more but the food should taste more delightful since you eat it off this earth-pan. One could order claypot rice, claypot fish, claypot meat, claypot noodle, etc. depending on what is available. The hawker would generally be of Chinese origin.

Glass bowls, each containing steamed or boiled red beans, sliced sweet potatoes, corn, water chestnut, black jelly, sago, coloured flour strips or balls, palm seeds, pineapple cubes, etc., mean a hot or cold variety of desserts is available. Sometimes coconut milk is added; sometimes brown sugar water is used; at other times evaporated milk tops the already sugar-syruped mix of nuts and beans. There are as many combinations as there are for milkshake flavours.

There are also other types of containers, cookers, fryers or mixers that tell what is sold. Likewise, **wrappings** convey the kind of desserts that have been prepared.

Glass drink containers

These are the local drink 'dispensers' except that everything is manual. There would normally be five or more cylindrical glass containers with liquids of various colours and levels. Sometimes an ice scraper may be noticed.

PREPARATION STYLES

The five food groups of Main Meal, Noodle, Snack, Dessert and Beverage would fall under one of several cooking methods. Let's coin up a few terms to pinpoint them:

Cooking Method

Style 1: In glass showcases.
Style 2: Over the charcoal.
Style 3: Slow steamed-done.
Style 4: Quick fried.
Style 5: Deep-oil fried.
Style 6: Ready-cooked food.
Style 7: Ice-cooled way.
Style 8: Keeping it warm.
Style 9: Special category.

So, what is in where now? Here's a list of some popular items grouped as per above headings. If you can just remember that 'M' stands for 'Main dish,' 'N' for 'Noodle,' 'D' for 'Dessert,' 'S' for 'Snack' and 'B' for 'Beverage' the list will not look more complicated than the food.

1:	**In glass showcases**		**Category**		**Thai script**	**page**
1.	Chinese Chicken Rice	M	*khao mun kai*		ข้าวมันไก่	29
2.	Red Roast Pork	M	*moo daeng*		หมูแดง	29
3.	Duck in Red Soy Sauce	M	*ped paloh*		เป็ดพะโล้	30
4.	Giblet Soup	M	*tue huan*		คือฮวน	30
5.	Thick Rice Soup (Congee)	M	*joak*		โจ๊ก	30
6.	Crispy Fish in Chillies	M	*yum pla duk foo*		ย้ำปลาดุกฟู	31
7.	Fishball Noodles	N	*kuay-tiao Luk-chin pla*		ก๋วยเตี๋ยวลูกชิ้นปลา	31
8.	Chicken Noodles	N	*kuay-tiao kai*		ก๋วยเตี๋ยวไก่	31
9.	Meatball Noodles	N	*kuay-tiao luk-chin nua*		ก๋วยเตี๋ยวลูกชิ้นเนื้อ	32
10.	Duck Noodles	N	*kuay-tiao ped*		ก๋วยเตี๋ยวเป็ด	32
11.	Noodles in Red Soup	N	*yen tao fo*		เย็นตาโฟ	32
12.	Noodles with Thick Vegetable Gravy	N	*kuay-tiao rad na*		ก๋วยเตี๋ยวราดหน้า	32
13.	Pan-Fried Noodles in Red Soy Sauce	N	*kuay tiao phad si iew*		ก๋วยเตี๋ยวผัดซีอิ๊ว	33
14.	Noodle Soup with Boiled Giblets	N	*kuay jub*		ก๋วยจั๊บ	33
15.	Egg Noodle Soup	N	*bah mee nam*		บะหมี่น้ำ	33
16.	Flour Pancake Rolls	S	*poh piah sod*		ปอเปี๊ยะสด	33
17.	Spicy Ground Beef	M	*larb nua*		ลาบเนื้อ	34
18.	Spicy Roast Beef Slices	M	*nam tok*		น้ำตก	34
19.	Papaya Salad	S	*som tam*		ส้มตำ	35
20.	Bamboo Shoot Salad	S	*sup nor mai*		ซุปหน่อไม้	35
21.	Five-star Roast Chicken	S	*kai yang ha dao*		ไก่ย่างห้าดาว	36
22.	Thai Style Sukiyaki	M	*sukiyaki*		สุกี้ยากี้	36
23.	Fried Rice	M	*khao phad*		ข้าวผัด	36
24.	Noodles on the boat	M	*kuay tiao rua*		ก๋วยเตี๋ยวเรือ	37
2:	**Over the charcoal**		**Category**			
1.	Barbecued Chicken/Pork	M	*kai yang/moo yang*		ไก่ย่าง-หมูย่าง	38
2.	Satay	S	*sateh*		สเต๊ก	38
3.	Roast Eggs	S	*khai ping*		ไข่ปิ้ง	39
4.	Thai Sausages	S	*sai krok*		ไส้กรอก	39
5.	Crispy Pancakes with Fillings	D	*khanom buang*		ขนมเบื้อง	39
6.	Indian Fried Pasta	D	*roti*		โรตี	40
7.	Tiny Pancakes with Fillings	D	*khanom tokyo*		ขนมโตเกียว	40

8.	Grilled Bananas	D	*kluay ping*	กล้วยปิ้ง	40
9.	Coconut Pudding	D	*khanom krok*	ขนมครก	41
10.	Roasted Sticky Rice in Banana Leaves	D	*khao niew ping*	ข้าวเหนียวปิ้ง	41
11.	Grilled Dry Squid	S	*pla muk ping*	ปลาหมึกปิ้ง	42
12.	Grilled Meat Balls	S	*luk chin ping*	ลูกชิ้นปิ้ง	42
13.	Roasted Sweet Potatoes	S	*mun ping*	มันปิ้ง	42
14.	Shredded Coconut Pudding	S	*khanom paeng jee*	ขนมแป้งจี่	43
15.	Chinese Waffles & Poorman's Pancakes	D	*khanom rang pung & Khanom tang taek*	ขนมรังผึ้ง ขนมถังแตก	43

3: Slow steamed-done Category

1.	Red-stewed Pork Legs	M	*kha moo paloh*	ขาหมูพะโล้	44
2.	Chinese Leaf-wrapped Glutinous Rice	M	*bah jang*	บ๊ะจ่าง	45
3.	Steamed Noodle Rolls	N	*kuay-tiao rod*	ก๋วยเตี๋ยวหลอด	46
4.	Pork Tapioca Balls	S	*sakoo sai moo*	สาคูไส้หมู	46
5.	Pork wrapped in Rice Pancakes	S	*khao kriab pak moh*	ข้าวเกรียบปากหม้อ	47
6.	Stuffed Vegetable inPuddongs	S	*khanom kui chai*	ขนมกุ้ยช่าย	47
7.	Chinese Dumplings	S	*khanom jeeb*	ขนมจีบ	47
8.	Chinese Steamed Buns	S	*salapao*	ซาลาเปา	48
9.	Steamed Nuts	S	*tua tom*	ถั่วต้ม	48
10.	Pumpkin Custard	D	*sangkaya fuk thong*	สังขยาฟักทอง	48
11.	Steamed Banana Cakes in Leaves	D	*khanom kluay*	ขนมกล้วย	49
12.	Steamed Sticky Rice in Banana Leaves	D	*khao tom mud*	ข้าวต้มมัด	42
13.	Shark's Fin Soup	M	*Hoo pla chalam*	หูปลาฉลาม	49

4: Quick-fried Category

1.	Fried Mussels in Batter	M	*hoy thod*	หอยทอด	50
2.	Fried Vegetable Puddings	S	*khanom kui chai thod*	ขนมกุ้ยช่ายทอด	51
3.	Thai Fried Noodles	N	*phad thai*	ผัดไทย	51
4.	A-la-carte dishes			อาหารตามสั่ง	51

5: Deep-oil fried Category

| 1. | Spring Rolls | S | *poh piah thod* | ปอเปี๊ยะทอด | 53 |

2.	Fried Wonton	S	kiew thod	เกี๊ยวทอด	53
3.	Fried Fish Cakes	S	thod mun pla	ทอดมันปลา	54
4.	Curry Puffs	S	kari pub	กะหรี่ปั๊บ	54
5.	Deep-Fried Locusts	S	tuktan thod	ตั๊กกะแตนทอด	54
6.	Fried Toast with Ground Pork/Shrimp	S	khanom pung na mou/kung	ขนมปังหน้าหมู/กุ้ง	55
7.	Fried Dough Balls	D	khanom khai hong	ขนมไข่หงษ์	55
8.	Fried Bananas	D	kluay kaek	กล้วยแขก	55
9.	Fried Potato Balls	D	khai nok kratha	ไข่นกกระทา	56
10.	Deep-fried Dough Sticks	S	pa thong koh	ปาท่องโก๋	56
11.	Fried Nut	S	tua thod	ถั่วทอด	56

6: Ready-cooked food   Category

1.	Fried Crab in Curry Sauce	M	pu phad pong kari	ปูผัดผงกระหรี่	57
2.	Fish Curry Cake in Banana Cup	M	hoh mok pla	ห่อหมกปลา	57
3.	Coconut Chicken Curry	M	kaeng kai	แกงไก่	58
4.	Beef/Chicken Curry with Peanuts	M	masaman nua/kai	มัสมั่น เนื้อ/ไก่	58
5.	Pork Rind Soup	M	kapoh pla	กระเพาะปลา	58
6.	Crispy Noodles	N	mee krob	หมี่กรอบ	59
7.	Red Noodles soaked in Coconut Milk	N	mee kati	หมี่กระทิ	59
8.	GoldenThreads/Egg Cakes	D	foi thong, thong yip, thong yod	ฝอยทอง, ทองหยิบ, ทองหยอด	59
9.	Tapioca Strings in Coconut Syrup	D	khanom pakrim kai tao	ปลากิมไข่เต่า	60
10.	Sticky Rice with Different Toppings	D	khao niew moon	ข้าวเหนียวมูล	60
11.	Boiled Bananas in Coconut Syrup	D	kluay buad chee	กล้วยบวดชี	60
12.	Flower-shaped Cookies	D	khanom dok lamduan	ขนมดอกลำดวน	61
13.	Desserts on the Wheel	D	Rod Khen/ Khanom Wann	รถเข็นขนมหวาน	61
14.	Fried Rice with Shrimp Paste	M	khao kluk kapi	ข้าวคลุกกะปิ	61

7: Ice-cooled way   Category

1.	Flour-dipped Chestnuts in Syrup	D	tub tim krob	ทับทิมกรอบ	62

2. Crushed-iced Sweets — D — *nam kaeng sai* — น้ำแข็งใส — 62
3. Black Jelly — D — *chao kuay* — เฉาก๊วย — 63
4. Sugar-cane Water — B — *nam oy* — น้ำอ้อย — 63
5. Longan Juice — B — *nam lamyai* — น้ำลำไย — 63
6. Fruit Juice — B — *nam pol-mai* — น้ำผลไม้ — 64
7. Local Ice Cream — 64
8. Singapore Green Strings — D — *lod chong Singapore* — ลอดช่องสิงคโปร์ — 64
9. Lotus Root Water — B — *nam rak bua* — น้ำรากบัว — 65
10. Green Leaf Water — B — *nam bai buabok* — น้ำใบบัวบก — 65
11. Chinese Herbal Water — B — *nam jub liang* — น้ำจับเลี้ยง — 65

8: Keeping it warm — Category

1. Bean Curd Milk — B — *nam tao hoo* — น้ำเต้าฮู้ — 66
2. Bird's Nest Soup — B — *rung nok* — รังนก — 66
3. Gingko Nut Soup — D — *pae kuay* — แปะก๊วย — 67

9: Special category — Category

1. Boiled Cockles — M — *hoy kraeng luak* — หอยแครงลวก — 68
2. Hot and Spicy Salad — S — *yum* — ยำ — 68
3. Thai Noodles with Fish Curry Sauce — N — *khanom-chine nam ya* — ขนมจีนน้ำยา — 69
4. Crispy Coconut and Tidbits — S — *miang khum* — เมี่ยงคำ — 69
5. Fresh Fruits — S — *pol-mai sod* — ผลไม้สด — 70
6. Preserved Fruits — S — *pol-mai dong* — ผลไม้ดอง — 70
7. Thai Cookies — S — *khanom ping* — ขนมผิง — 70
8. Chinese Cakes with Filling — S — *khanom piah* — ขนมเปี๊ยะ — 71
9. Sweet Silk Threads with Flour Pancakes — D — *roti sai mai* — โรตีสายไหม — 71
10. Banana in Syrup — D — *kluay chuam* — กล้วยเชื่อม — 71
11. Tapioca Balls in Coconut Syrup — D — *bua loy* — บัวลอย — 71
12. Mock Miniature Fruit — D — *luk chub* — ลูกชุบ — 72
13. Bean - filled Crescents — D — *khanom tua paeb* — ขนมถั่วแปบ — 72
14. Chewy Strings — D — *khanom niew* — ขนมเหนียว — 72
15. Crispy Rolls — D — *thong muan* — ทองม้วน — 72
16. Coconut Pudding in Banana Leaf Cups — D — *tako* — ตะโก้ — 73
17. Layer Cake — D — *khanom chan* — ขนมชั้น — 73
18. Boiled Rice with Delicacies — M — *khaotom kui* — ข้าวต้มกุ๊ย — 73

TIPS TO THE TABLE

No, we are not ready to eat yet! A few more pointers might be in order so that a meal can truly be enjoyed.

Varieties of Thai Hawker Food come by the score and there is even variety within a variety offering an endless opportunity for experience and enjoyment. It depends on whether the hawker is a 'Bangkokian,' or from the North, Northeast or South; on whether he is a 'Chinese Thai' or a 'Thai Thai'! And, for that matter, whether he is a Muslim Thai. Indian-Thais do not take to hawking except for selling fried nuts, carried in a 'school-desk' table on the head.

This craziness happily offers an escape route for the shy tourist since there are so many versions of the same thing. At worst, you can console yourself privately and say "Ha, I want it **this** way, so what? The customer is never wrong."

Failing everything else simply point and say: *nee, nee, nee...*(*nee* = 'this') 'soup' with a broad thankful smile to complement your gesture.

Most hawkers do not speak English at all but will be only too pleased to hawk that extra bowl of soup for you. Nearly all will understand the word 'soup' which has become a part of the local culinary vocabulary. Usually, one may sit anywhere where there is a vacant chair. Sometimes, hawkers will not allow non-diners to their food to sit on their precious chairs and eat others'cooking. It is therefore best to ascertain if 'I may sit here' first.

Where there is no free table, feel free to share one. Probably before long, both parties would be laughing away. It happens everyday.

One handy Thai word to note is *aroy* for 'delicious.' Even among locals one inadvertently asks the diner *aroy mai?* (*aroy*=delicious; *mai*= or not). The normal polite answer is *aroy mak* (very delicious).

Thais generally eat their food accompanied by plain water, usually with ice cubes or crushed ice. This reaches the point of being 'automatic' with some hawkers who will place a glass of it without being asked, after he has placed the ordered food in front of you. If none is provided and you want to go local all the way, say in a low tone *narm kaeng plao*. Refer to the glossary for some easy phrases.

One local feature: pretend not to be surprised when you find a big bowl thrust unto you which is but only half or three quarters full! This appears to be daylight robbery but it is to allow for easy mixing of condiments. (Hard to justify for the half glass of 'car-fe' or hot coffee.)

It makes sense not to hand out a 500 baht banknote for a 20 baht meal. Often, the long wait for return change can spoil what otherwise would have been an enjoyable meal. Don't frustrate yourself!

STUCK-UP HAWKERS

'Stone - deaf ' people

No, they are not deaf in the least, but as it happens daily, we have to include this paragraph to alert you so that you can take out your frustration on the washing machine when you go home.

While it may not happen so often to Caucasians as to Asians, some hawkers appear to be utterly deaf, totally disinterested and utterly unaware of your presence. There is no milder way to describe them! Well, don't be offended if he or she appears not even to hear you.He/she probably does but very often, the hawker simply seems to ignore an order, looking stiffer than a zombie. Compose yourself, go nose-to-nose to him, roll your eyeballs and repeat the order; but don't touch his nose. This is molestation in Thailand!

Shallow-memory 'waiters'

Then there is this other type, whether he is the waiting boy, serving girl or cooking boss: they seem to forget inside sixty seconds what you had just ordered. You may also experience the annoyance of seeing later arrivals being served ahead of you, or, some other waiter or the same person will come up to you and ask what you had ordered.

Just repeat - if you can remember - and, if possible, put on your most insincere smile and enjoy the whole episode. Call it 'experience' when you are home. We call it 'way of life.'

But try not to walk out in a show of temper. This, in Thailand, is uncultured behaviour. Patience and tolerance are essential dining ingredients in this country. Besides, how else can one enjoy another's cooking?

TAKE - AWAY PACKET

There are always facilities for a take-away, *sai tung* [put in (a) bag], if joining a herd at the table is not your cup of tea. The vendor will use a plastic bag for this though the more modern hawkers may have polyform trays.

The condiment, usually chilli - dried or in vinegar and sugar is separately prepared in a little bag all rubber-banded up.

For noodles with soup, the soup will be housed in yet another bag.

Whether eating alfresco or taking home, the very same dish will come in the ordinary version or, for 5 baht more, a special which has more noodles and more ingredients, sometimes the 'special' being just an egg and two pieces of tissue-thin meat. To order anything special, just say : *phi-set* otherwise the ordinary *thummada* is assumed.

To order only the ingredients without any noodles at all, say *kao lao*.

Here's a more practical way for you. Point to the hawker as required :

Take - away *(sai tung)*	1. ใส่ถุง
Special *(phi - set)*	2. พิเศษ
Ordinary *(thummada)*	3. ธรรมดา
Soup *(nam)*	4. น้ำ
Dry *(haeng)*	5. แห้ง
Broad noodles *(sen yai)*	6. เส้นใหญ่
Small noodles *(sen lek)*	7. เส้นเล็ก
Rice vermicelli *(sen mee)*	8. เส้นหมี่
Bean vermicelli *(woon sen)*	9. วุ้นเส้น
Egg noodles *(bah mee)*	10. บะหมี่
Chicken *(kai)*	11. ไก่
Beef *(nua)*	12. เนื้อ
Pork *(moo)*	13. หมู
Without noodles *(kao lao)*	14. เกาเหลา
Two packets *(song tung)*	15. สองถุง
Three packets *(sarm tung)*	16. สามถุง

If you can commit to memory these simple phrases, you can order practically every rice, noodle and snack item quite easily. Or make photocopies of them and tick them off and hand it to the vendor as you would for a prescription.

THE EXPERIENCE IS IN THE EATING

One (mis)conception to hawkers' food is that most of them are unhygienic. This depends on one's outlook and sophistication but undeniably there is bound to be some litter on the floor, squeaky chairs, terrible looking display of chicken, heaps of unwashed plates and maybe uncovered condiment bottles.

Still, if millions of locals are happily gobbling down hawker fare daily, surely it would not be that clinically disastrous for a visitor to have a go, just for once, or more times?

The precaution perhaps is not to consume too much too often but to go easy on the stomach until it is 'seasoned' as the saying goes. A good thing to do is perhaps not to eat anything too spicy on a very empty stomach and then flood everything with very cold drinks. Even a strong stomach wall can have weak muscles.

A good idea is to have some tissues handy so that chopsticks and spoons can be given a wiping, if this will make you feel happier. The tissue will also come in well for your nostrils when the food is too pungent or too delicious.

The food will come hot or steaming so it is only prudent to relax and go slow so that the first spoonful will not scorch the tongue. This would then be a good start to get the full tantalising sensation of Thai Hawker Food.

NOW we are ready to tuck in, once we have selected something from the broad spectrum of the hawkers' delights.

1.1 Chinese Chicken Rice
Khao Mun Kai ข้าวมันไก่

Boiled chicken appears on the dining tables of many nation-
alities. The Hainanese dish is, however, unique for the
steamed rice that is served with it. The rice is cooked with
chicken stock reserved from the boiled chicken. When
served, the chicken is sliced into pieces and arranged, either
on top of the rice or on a separate serving plate, with
cucumber and, sometimes, tomato. It is served with a
special sauce which has a mixture of soy sauce, soy bean
paste, minced ginger roots and chillies.

1.2. Red - Roast Pork
Moo Daeng หมูแดง

For those who have been to the Orient or Chinatown in a
western country, a rail from which long strips of red roast
pork are hung is a common sight. Red roast pork is a
traditional favourite Chinese dish among not only native
people but also people in other parts of the world. When
served, the pork, brushed with red food colouring during the
roasting, is sliced and taken with rice or topped on egg
noodles, thus becoming egg noodles with roast pork *bah
mee moo daeng*. Red-roast pork is usually displayed with
roast duck at most stalls or in foodshops.

1.3. Duck in Red Soy Sauce
Ped Paloh   เป็ดพะโล้

The Chinese are noted for their art of cooking ducks. The world-renowned 'Peking duck' strongly substantiates this acclaim.

This dish of duck in red soy sauce, however, tastes differently from the Peking duck. The meat of the stewed duck is tender and it is commonly served with rice. When sliced and put in a bowl of noodle soup. it becomes duck noodle soup *kuay-tiao ped.*   ก๋วยเตี๋ยวเป็ด

1.4. Giblet Soup
Tue Huan   ตือฮวน

Apart from livers, Westerners hardly take into consideration the nourishment of giblets, not to mention cooking them for their meals. When clean and cooked properly, giblets are no less tasty than meat. Giblet soup is, for example, one of the delicious dishes easily found on the roadside. Boiled giblets of different kinds are displayed on a strainer, which is usually put on top of a huge bowl of boiling soup. Some like to take the soup with steamed rice.

1.5. Thick Rice Soup
Joak   โจ๊ก

This Chinese dish is usually served either for breakfast or supper. The soup, creamy and thick after several hours of cooking, is added with ground pork shaped into small balls, liver and sometimes kidney or chicken shreds or fish according to your order. An egg may be added to it if you want. It comes with a topping of onion shoots and chopped string onion. It is served in individual bowls and often taken with *pa thong koh.*

1.6. Crispy Fish in Chillies
Yum Pla Duk Foo ยำปลาดุกฟู

This hot and spicy fish salad, found in the menu of nearly every Thai restaurant, is also available at some hawker stalls which sell a variety of Thai take-home food. The secret of this dish lies in the preparation of the fish, *pla duk,* which is steamed, crushed and deep-fried before it is mixed with chillies, lemon juice, fish sauce and red onions.

1.7. Fishball Noodles
Kuay-tiao Luk-chin Pla ก๋วยเตี๋ยวลูกชิ้นปลา

A pile of white fishballs and a variety of noodles rice noodles, egg noodles, rice vermicelli and bean vermicelli are prominently displayed at these stalls. You can choose the noodles you like to go with the fishballs, and your noodle bowl can be with or without soup. With stock added to your bowl, you will end up enjoying the noodles, fishballs and the delicious soup.

Besides fishballs, some hawkers also include pork noodles in their showcases. You can have the noodles, either dry or with soup, with pork and giblets.

1.8. Chicken Noodles
Kuay-tiao Kai ก๋วยเตี๋ยวไก่

Prominently displayed in the showcase are boiled chickens, either hung whole from a bar or sliced into pieces. The only main ingredient for this dish, besides noodles, is sliced chicken. You can order dried noodles or noodle soups, and there are rice and egg noodles. Some hawkers also offer steamed rice as an alternative to noodles, so you can order a dish of chicken rice if noodles are not your cup of tea.

1.9. Meatball Noodles
Kuay-tiao Luk-chin Nua ก๋วยเตี๋ยวลูกชิ้นเนื้อ

Apart from meatballs, you can choose fresh beef slices, stewed beef or beef giblets for your bowl of dried noodles or noodle soup. While pork stock made the soup of fishball noodles, beef stock is in the meatball noodle bowl.

1.10. Duck Noodles
Kuay-tiao Ped ก๋วยเตี๋ยวเป็ด

The dish looks simple—duck slices topped on noodles but its secret is in the stock. One can tell if a hawker is 'professional' in preparing the duck noodle soup by judging from the stock, which has a combination of duck bones, soy sauce and spices all simmering for at least a few hours.

1.11. Noodles in Red Soup
Yen Tao Fo เย็นตาโฟ

A large variety of items put in this soup includes cuttlefish, fishballs, fried bean curd, pork, bloodcakes and 'morning glory' (local) vegetable. The soup is unique for its red colour, resulting from salted soy bean paste. Many hawkers, however, do not bother about the authentic paste and take the short cut of mixing red colour with water and flour to be put in the soup. In Hongkong, Singapore and Malaysia, the soup is plain (without the red tinge)

1.12. Noodles with thick Vegetable Gravy
Kuay-tiao Rad Na ก๋วยเตี๋ยวราดหน้า

Cooking a noodle dish is less time-consuming compared to other main dishes. This is the reason why noodle stalls are omnipresent on the city's sidewalks. This is another easy dish that takes only a few minutes to cook.

Noodles are stir-fried first and topped with a thick gravy of vegetable. Pork (beef, prawns or seafood), soybean paste and fish sauce, usually fried separately are then lopped on top.

1.13. Pan-Fried Noodles in Red Soy Sauce
Kuay-tiao Phad Si Ew　ก๋วยเตี๋ยวผัดซีอิ๊ว

This and the preceding dish are like twins. At a stall where *kuay-tiao rad na* is served, this dish of pan-fried noodles is also available. This is, however, a dry dish in which noodles are pan-fried with vegetable and pork for a few minutes before they are sprinkled with a few drops of red soy sauce, fish sauce and a dash of sugar.

1.14. Noodle Soup with Boiled Giblets
Kuay Jub　ก๋วยจั๊บ

People in many Asian countries find giblets nutritious, so they can be found in nearly every market. For this dish, pork giblets are boiled and sliced into pieces to be put in the noodle soup, which is available either in clear pork broth or in soy sauce gravy.

1.15. Egg Noodle Soup
Bah Mee Nam　บะหมี่น้ำ

Though egg noodles can usually be found and ordered at most noodle stalls, there are some hawkers who specialise in egg noodles and wontons. At these *bah mee / kieo* (egg noodles and wontons) stalls, you won't see any white noodles but yellowish egg noodles and wontons with several strips of red roast pork or crab meat. You can choose to top the noodles with sliced roast pork or crab meat, and the noodles can be dry or with soup.

1.16. Flour Pancake Rolls
Poh Piah Sod　ปอเปี๊ยะสด

Flour pancake rolls are perfect hors d'oeuvres mainly because of their light ingredients. The filling, which has a combination of boiled beansprouts, pork, pork sausages and sliced omelette, is wrapped in thin pancakes made of rice flour. The rolls are topped with a sauce mixture of cornstarch and soy sauce.

1.17. Spicy Ground Beef Northeastern Style
Larb Nua ลาบเนื้อ

A traditional dish of Northeastern Thailand, unofficially called *I-saan*, the outstanding character of this dish is its strong taste and flavour. Northeasterners love hot food! Foreigners including many Asian visitors find this dish tongue burning but it is not impossible to like it. If you are not familiar with hot food, you can simply tell the hawker to reduce the amount of chillies since it is usually prepared individually.

Have you seen a hawker indulging in pounding something in a mortar with a pestle? If yes, walk closer and take a look. *Larb nua* is often one of the dishes available at this particular stall where many other northeastern dishes are also served.

1.18. Spicy Roast Beef Slices
Nam Tok น้ำตก

Another favourite dish from Northeastern Thailand, *nam tok* (literally meaning 'waterfall'), has an anecdote to its name. In the cooking process, beef is grilled and the flowing liquid, or waterfall, is saved to mix with the beef slices together with other ingredients including chillies, lemon juice, sliced red onions and roast paddy powder.

Today, hawkers are too busy to stand in front of a hot stove to collect the dripping liquid from the beef, so the 'waterfall' is no longer added!

The stove is also used for cooking a few other northeastern Thai dishes including grilled beef liver *tup yang* and roast beef *nua yang*. Apart from roasting, that same stove is used for boiling beef giblet soup *kruang nai tom*. Hawkers don't have too much space for too many stoves, mind you.

1.19. Papaya Salad
Som Tam ส้มตำ

A traditional dish of Northeastern Thailand, this deadly hot salad of sliced papaya strings is a favourite to Thai people in every part of the country. Instead of a mixing bowl called for in Western salad, papaya salad is always mixed in a mortar with a pestle. If you see this pair of kitchen utensils at a hawker stall, it's probable that *som tam* is sold there. Believe it or not, those who love to burn their tongues and torture their mouths can ask a hawker to put at least 10 chillies in the salad.

Because a dish of papaya salad is inexpensive, it can be the lunch even for a big-appetite worker who normally eats it with steamed glutinous rice. Papaya salad is one of the most favourite foods of a large number of migrant workers from Thailand's Northeast.

This is also a 'poor man's food', so it is not unusual to see a hawker, surrounded by a throng of customers, sitting on a mat at an open space or in front of a gas station and indulging in pounding the salad. A steamer for glutinous rice is always at his side.

1.20. Bamboo Shoot Salad
Sup Nor Mai ซุปหน่อไม้

Apart from papaya salad, the same mortar and pestle are also useful for mixing bamboo shoot salad, also a Northeastern dish. The taste of bamboo shoot salad is not the same as papaya salad, since it calls for different ingredients though they are both hot. The bamboo shoot strings are mixed with powdery roasted rice, lemon juice and fish sauce.

If you have never had this food but want to try it, take a small portion to be on the safe side.

1.21. Five-star Roast Chicken
Kai Yang Ha Dao   ไก่ย่างห้าดาว

This is a chain hawker food which can be found at nearly every street of Bangkok particularly at busy shopping complexes or supermarkets. Every stall is displayed with a logo of a chicken and five stars. The taste of five-star chicken is however similar to other roast chickens sold on sidewalks. Instead of roasting the chickens on charcoal, the chicken are prominently grilled in a gas-fuelled stove inside which they can be clearly seen. The stove serves more or less as a showcase.

1.22. Thai-style Sukiyaki
Sukiyaki   สุกี้-ยากี้

The name is Japanese but a Japanese can hardly tell if this is their traditional dish if he has a bite. The original Japanese name is maintained but the cooking method has changed in such a way that it has nothing similar to the original *sukiyaki* of Japan. Some Japanese like the *Thai sukiyaki* though, saying it is tasty potpourri. The *Thai sukiyaki* gives a choice of pork, beef, chicken, shrimps and cuttlefish. Other ingredients consist of vermicelli, vegetables and eggs.

1.23. Fried Rice
Khao Phad   ข้าวผัด

Fried rice with pork	*khao phad moo*	ข้าวผัดหมู
Fried rice with chicken	*khao phad kai*	ข้าวผัดไก่
Fried rice with shrimp	*khao phad kung*	ข้าวผัดกุ้ง

Ordinary white rice, already pre-cooked, is the main ingredient.

This is a Main Dish as it is very filling and the variation lies in whether pork, chicken or shrimp is used. Often, shrimp is added to the pork or chicken. Sometimes crab meat is also used.

The addition of egg is taken for granted, since without, it lacks taste and as this dish is intended as one of the two or three main meals of a day, hawkers always add the egg to it. Fried rice is served with cucumber slices, salad greens and raw onion shoots.

1.24. Noodles on the Boat
Kuay Tiao Rua   ก๋วยเตี๋ยวเรือ

It is sometimes hard for a foreign visitor to understand why a hawker has to put his noodle pots and all the ingredients in a boat, and place the boat on the roadside. A brief explanation to this practice is that in the old days, many vendors paddled their boats along canals or rivers to sell food and merchandise.

As many rivers and canals are filled up in the name of urban development, paddling vendors went ashore. Noodle vendors have maintained their 'trademark' by keeping the boat.

There are two main kinds of noodles on the boat: pork and beef.

2
OVER
THE
CHARCOAL

2.1. Barbecued Chicken/Pork
Kai Yang, Moo Yang   ไก่ย่าง-หมูย่าง

This type of roadside fast-food entices at every corner of Bangkok's streets. It is popular among pedestrians who simply point at what they want and pay, so no problem of language barrier. Most Thais like to take the barbecued chicken or pork with steamed glutinous rice and chilli sauce, which are also available at the stall.

2.2. Satay Beef, Chicken, Pork
Sateh, Nua, Kai, Moo   สเต๊ก, เนื้อ, ไก่, หมู

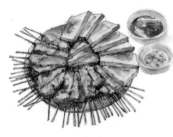

No definite line can be drawn on whether satay is a snack or main dish. Again, it cannot be clearly determined if satay is for lunch, dinner or supper; it's too heavy for breakfast, of course. Most people like to order a dish of satay to sooth the stomach before the main course. It is however not against etiquette (What's the etiquette of sidewalk eating anyway?) to adhere to satay until you are full if you deeply love it.

dishes: one the satay sauce which has a mixture of dried chillies, peanuts, coconut milk and curry paste, and the other a mixture of cucumber slices, chillies, vinegar and sugar.

2.3. Roasted Eggs
Khai Ping ไข่ปิ้ง

Another poor man's favourite (Does a poor man have many choices?), roasted eggs are simple as the name says. Fresh chicken eggs (chicken is emphasized here because people in this country also eat duck eggs) are put on a rack over a charcoal oven and roasted until done. A hawker usually offers soy sauce with the egg. A roasted egg is sold at 3-5 baht.

2.4. Thai Sausages
Sai Krok ไส้กรอก

The appearance of Thai sausages is not so different from that of Western sausages but the tastes are worlds apart. Ingredients in their fillings are different and Thai sausages are rather spicy. There are beef and pork sausages, *sai krok nua* and *sai krok moo* respectively, and the fillings are more or less the same except for the meat. Other ingredients in the sausages include glutinous rice, minced ginger, pepper and salt. There are also rice sausages, *sai krok khao* (*khao* meaning rice), inside which meat is omitted. All sausages are grilled only and served with some vegetables.

2.5. Crispy Pancakes with Fillings
Khanom Buang ขนมเบื้อง

Thai crispy pancakes which look very much like Mexican tacos are omnipresent on most sidewalks where a hawker is seen spreading batter on a flat-bottomed pan with a spatula. Coconut cream is topped on the pancake before fillings are placed on it. The two different fillings from which one can choose are the sweet filling: containing shredded coconut and golden threads (egg yolk strips) and the salty filling: having shredded coconut and chopped spring onions. Spreading the pancake is easy in the eyes of most people. In fact it is an art which needs an experienced person; thus goes a Thai saying: Do not spread *khanom buang* with your mouth.

2.6. Indian Pastry (Indian Fried Pastry)
Roti โรตี

Indian immigrants in Thailand introduced this traditional dessert to people in Thailand decades ago and it has become a favourite dessert in this country ever since. The art of making the pastry has, however, been passed on through several generations, and Thai hawkers—mostly with Indian or Muslim origin—are good at making this dessert. The fried pastry is spread with butter and sprinkled with sweet milk and sugar before it is rolled with a piece of white paper.

2.7. Tiny Pancakes with Fillings
Khanom Tokyo ขนมโตเกียว

The name *Khanom Tokyo* gives an impression that the Japanese capital is related to this sidewalk dessert but its origin remains obscure. The pancakes are normally about two to three inches in diameter and the fillings range from sausages to mashed taro and crushed beans.

2.8. Grilled Bananas
Kluay Ping กล้วยปิ้ง

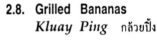

This is a very simple dessert which does not need any sophisticated preparation: simply peel a banana and grill it on a charcoal oven. A kind of local banana, called *kluay nam wa*, is good for this grilling method. On the same oven, one may see unpeeled bananas grilled side by side to the peeled ones. A different kind of banana, called *kluay huk muk,* is used for this purpose. Some hawkers grill the peeled bananas as they are while some cut a banana into four pieces and thread the slices on barbecue sticks.

2.9. Coconut Pudding
Khanom Krok ขนมครก

The traditional way of making coconut puddings is so exquisite that it is an unarguable art in itself. Watching a hawker preparing every single pudding is entertaining. It starts with slowly pouring the batter into each little hole of a round pan to be followed by sweet coconut milk. Every hole is then covered individually and the mixture is baked on a charcoal stove for several minutes.

The world today is however too busy for those fine details. What you see at most sidewalk stalls nowadays is a quick version of the baking process, of which a hawker is normally seen pouring the batter from a kettle into the pan holes and covering them with a single big cover until the puddings are baked. Charcoal stoves still exist at some stalls but most hawkers prefer baking the puddings on gas stoves.

2.10. Roast / Steamed Sticky Rice in Banana Leaves
Khao Niew Ping, Khao Tom Mud
ข้าวเหนียวปิ้ง, ข้าวต้มมัด

The rapid urbanisation of Thailand has seen less and less banana trees. Banana leaves are also becoming scarce but many hawkers continue to hold on to the traditional way of cooking by using banana leaves to wrap food in order to get the aroma. Sticky rice in banana leaves is one of the good examples of the fight for survival of the old tradition. Many kinds of Thai food which need banana leaves have been adapted to avoid having to use them, but never with these desserts.

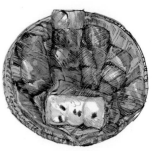

Sticky rice, with fillings of bananas, shredded coconut or mashed taro, is wrapped with banana leaves after which they can be either steamed or grilled. Luckily enough, most hawkers still grill them with charcoal ovens.

2.11. Grilled Dry Squid
Pla Muk Ping ปลาหมึกปิ้ง

Grilled fresh squids are usually available at seafood restaurants where food prices are more expensive than those on sidewalks. Dry squids, grilled over nothing else but the charcoal, are however widely known as a favourite street food. Apart from a tiny charcoal stove, another necessary utensil for this type of snack is a 'squid pressing device' needed to press a grilled dry squid. After being pressed, the paper-thin grilled squid is sticky and chewy but bland, so a sauce of mixed chillies, peanuts and syrup is always served with it.

Most hawkers display dry squids of various sizes at their stalls so that the customer can choose the one he wants. The bigger the dry squid, the dearer the price.

2.12. Grilled Meatballs
Luk Chin Ping ลูกชิ้นปิ้ง

It is in fact unnecessary to explain, even to a new visitor to Thailand, how grilled meatballs appear at a hawker stall. The sight of it is clear in itself. Grilled meatballs, of which a few meatballs are pierced on a barbecue stick, are traditionally grilled on a charcoal stove but nowadays some hawkers resort to the time-saving method of deep-frying them. The tastes of grilled and deep-fried meatballs are slightly different, of course. After they are grilled, the meatballs are dipped in chilli sauce, so ask the hawker to omit the sauce if you think it is too hot for you.

2.13. Roasted Potatoes
Mun Ping มันปิ้ง

Hawkers never limit their 'invention for survival' to just one kind of food. Sidewalk gourmets should not be surprised to see them selling more than one item at a single stall. Potatoes, for example, are always roasted on a rack over the charcoal with several other snacks including eggs, bananas and tapioca. Local potatoes for roasting are bigger than and taste different from cooking potatoes. Eggs, bananas and potatoes, when roasted, are eaten plain but roasted tapioca is usually dipped in syrup and roasted again before being served.

2.14. Shredded Coconut Puddings
Khanom Paeng Jee   ขนมแป้งจี่

Watching a vendor baking this dessert over a flat-bottomed pan is fun for it is very much like child's play. The pudding can be as small as one centimetre in diametre, or bigger in size but normally no larger than 2.5 cm in diameter. Major ingredients are glutinous rice flour, shredded coconut and palm sugar. The ingredients are mixed with a small amount of water and kneaded until smooth. In baking them, the vendor drops a spoon of the pudding on to a pan. The puddings are sold at eight or four pieces per baht depending on their size.

2.15. Chinese Waffles & Poorman's Pancakes
Khanom Rang Pung & Khanom Tang
Taek   ขนมรังผึ้ง & ขนมถังแตก

The shape and appearance of Chinese waffles are similar to their Western counterpart, but the taste is slightly different. Butter and milk do not exist in the ingredients of Chinese waffles.

Together with waffles, some hawkers also bake *Khanom tang taek*, literally meaning pancake for a broke man, at the same stall. The batter of the poorman's pancakes has a mixture of flour and eggs and they are topped with shredded coconut, suger and sesame seeds. To make full use of a vending stall, some hawkers also add another Thai pastry, *Khanom fuk bua* — a round-shaped dough deep-fried in a pan.

3
SLOW
STEAMED
DONE

3.1. Red - Stewed Pork
Legs Kha Moo Paloh   ขาหมูพะโล้

Many of the hawker foods in Bangkok are of Chinese origin; this dish is one of them. Though many hawkers prefer to offer a variety of food in a single stall, some stick to nothing else but this dish. Displayed at the stall are entire pork legs soaked in simmering red sauce, in a large basin or wok. The red sauce, a popular Chinese cooking element, is made up of dark sauce and flavouring spices.

When hard-boiled eggs are dipped in the gravy for several minutes, they become 'soy-eggs' *khai paloh*, and are served with pork leg slices and rice, often with some boiled greens.

3.2. Chinese Leaf - Wrapped Glutinous Rice
Bah Jang ป๊ะจ่าง

This Chinese version of tamales is traditionally made during the annual Dragon Boat Race but, in Thailand, you don't have to wait until the festival to enjoy this particular food. The outstanding characteristic of this dish is the *ti* leaves which are used to wrap a mixture of glutinous rice and a variety of other ingredients including dried shrimps, peanuts, Chinese sausage, mushroom, salted eggs and pork.

Bah jang is in fact specially made during the fifth moon of the Chinese calender, but its popularity among taste buds in Thailand has led the money-conscious hawker to sell these goodies almost all year round. Whether on roadsides or in food-shops, *bah jang* is always wrapped in *ti* leaves and steamed in a steamer before it is served. You can spot this item by its triangular wrapping with a straw string tied all round it. Sometimes a bundle is hung up for display as well.

An interesting legend behind this mouth-watering dish has it that *bah jang* represented the main food in the Boat Dragon Festival, originated by an emperor in honour of his favourite knight who drowned himself in the river. The knight was loyal to the emperor and unfortunately became extremely jealous of the emperor's only son who successfully executed a plot whereby the knight was accused of being a traitor.

Because the emperor dearly loved the knight, he commanded that his beloved 'friend' be banished from the kingdom instead of the tough traditional punishment of execution. The knight decided that he would rather die than have to live in exile. He drowned himself in the river and his spirit visited the emperor that very night to tell him of his innocence. The grief-stricken emperor then asked his subjects to throw food into the river to feed the knight. The food was wrapped in *ti* leaves to avoid being soaked by water. The emperor also ordered boats to cruise up and down the river, thus the Boat Festival, to chase away evil spirits and so let the knight enjoy his meal.

3.3. Steamed Noodle Rolls
Kuay-tiao Lord ก๋วยเตี๋ยวหลอด

The Chinese belief of eating uncut noodles for longevity— long strands to lengthen the span of one's life – cannot apply to this noodle dish since rice noodle dough is spread in a sheet instead of into strands. The noodle dough, called 'fun' in Cantonese (hence 'chee cheong fun' as in Singapore or Hong Kong), is sprinkled with tiny dried shrimps, so don't mistake them for chillies. Then they are rolled and steamed. When served, the noodle rolls are cut into pieces, and topped with boiled beansprouts, fried garlic and dark soy sauce.

In another recipe, the noodle dough is wrapped in a square shape over the filling of boiled pork or shrimps and strips of bamboo shoots, and steamed.

3.4. Pork Tapioca Balls
Sakoo Sai Moo สาคูไส้หมู

When you spot a small steamer with a cone-shaped cover at a roadside stall, it is possible the hawker is selling this snack. The dough, consisting of tiny tapioca pellets and water, is kneaded and shaped into balls, covering the filling of minced pork and peanuts. The balls are steamed and served with coriander and lettuce leaves.

THAI HAWKER FOOD

3.5. Pork Wrapped in Rice Pancakes
Khao Kriab Pak Moh ข้าวเกรียบปากหม้อ

The filling for this pancake has similar ingredients as that of pork tapioca balls; so it is not unusual to see the two snacks sold at the same stall. The way a hawker makes the thin and transparent rice pancakes on a steamer is unique and interesting.

It takes an experienced hawker less than a minute to make a pancake starting from spreading the batter into thin pancake over a steamer to putting in the filling and wrapping it. Watching the cooking process is entertaining; having a bite of it is irresistible!

3.6. Stuffed Vegetable Puddings
Khanom Kui Chai ขนมกุ้ยช่าย

Another type of sidewalk fast food, these Chinese puddings can be easily grabbed from a hawker. Though categorised as a snack, only a few pieces of the pudding is sufficient for a budgetary meal. In addition to vegetables, the puddings are also stuffed with other fillings, including diced bamboo shoots mixed with dried shrimps, sliced lettuces, sliced taro, etc. The puddings are either steamed or pan-fried, and served with soy sauce.

3.7. Chinese Dumplings
Khanom Jip ขนมจีบ

Widely known as '*siu mai*' in Chinese, it is common to see hawkers selling these steamed meat dumplings together with steamed buns, which are always kept warm in a steamer. *Khanom jip* is truly an all-time favourite among the Thais and Chinese alike and is taken with other dumplings as in a "*dim-sum*" lunch.

3.8. Chinese Steamed Buns
Salapao   ซาลาเปา

Known as '*cha siu bow*' in Cantonese dialect, fillings for the buns vary from barbecued pork to minced pork with bamboo shoots, mashed yellow mung beans and mashed black beans. Dumplings and hot steamed buns are two of the *dim-sum* items found at hawker stalls or in Chinese restaurants.

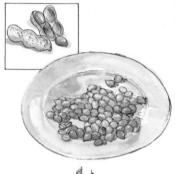

3.9. Boiled Nuts / Fried Nuts
Tua Tom, Tua Thod   ถั่วต้ม, ถั่วทอด

These snacks are very simple and straightforwardly cooked. Fondly called 'poor man's snacks', peanuts, roasted or boiled, are cheap both to consumers and for a hawker's investment. Unshelled peanuts can be boiled or roasted, while shelled nuts of various kinds such as peanuts and cashew nuts are roasted and sprinkled with salt. Nuts, however cooked, are rich in protein.

3.10. Coconut and Pumpkin Custard
Sangkaya Fuk Thong   สังขยาฟักทอง

Coconut milk, a common ingredient in a Thai kitchen, makes the custard taste different from that of the West. Coconut custard *sangkaya* is one of the favourite desserts for most Thais. It can be eaten plain but most people prefer taking it with sticky rice. The custard, which also has the mixture of eggs and sugar, is sometimes filled in a pumpkin (thus pumpkin custard) or coconut (coconut custard) and steamed.

3.11. Steamed Banana Cakes in Leaves
Khanom Kluay ขนมกล้วย

Bananas are boiled and crushed before they are mixed with coconut and a little flour. The mixture is then wrapped in banana leaves and steamed.

At a stall where this dessert is sold, you can see many other desserts in which banana leaves are involved. Banana leaves, when steamed, give a pleasant smell and, when wrapped and folded into cups, are practical food containers. Besides banana cakes, banana leaves are also widely used to hold palm cakes khanom tarn, coconut-filled puddings *khanom sord* sai and taro cakes *khanom puak*. However, some hawkers use ceramic cups instead of banana leaf cups for these desserts.

3.12. Steamed Sticky Rice In Banana Leaves
Khao Tom Mud ข้าวต้มมัด

See (page 42 Cagetory 2.10)

3.13. Shark's Fin Soup
Hoo Pla Chalam หูปลาฉลาม

Though thread-like shark's fin is expensive, do not be surprised when you see this delicacy on the roadside. After all, roadside food is not restricted for the poorman. Because shark's fin soup is one of the most favourite and expensive Chinese ingredients, it is mostly served in restaurants. However, in many areas of Bangkok especially in Chinatown, or Yaowaraj Road, there are many pick-up trucks which are converted into roadside resturants serving mainly shark's fin soup.

Chinese people believe that shark's fin, which takes at least five days to be soaked and become transparent, is rich in vitamins and calcium.

4
QUICK
FRIED

4.1. Fried Mussels in Batter
Hoy Thod หอยทอด

Mussels are cooked and served in many ways either as main dishes or hors d'oeuvre. Steamed mussels with chilli sauce, for example, make a favourite dish. Some shops or stalls exclusively sell fried mussels while a few add other pan-fried dishes to give eaters more choice. Since fresh mussels are available in Thailand all year round, particularly during the rainy season (July- Oct.), filling the stomach with this dish is easy.

The batter, a mixture of tapioca flour, cornstarch, salt, water and, of course, shelled mussels, is fried together with scrambled eggs on a flat-bottomed pan the most important utensil to cook this dish. It is topped with beansprouts, sprinkled with chopped coriander and green onion, and served with chilli sauce.

When you see a hawker indulging in the 'art of frying batter' in front of a huge frying pan, with a bowl of batter at the side, step in... order a dish of '*hoy thod*' and you won't be dissappointed.

4.2. Fried Vegetable Puddings
Khanom Kui Chai Thod
ขนมกุ๋ยช่ายทอด

This type of food, or snack to be more specific, is of Chinese origin. The puddings can be stuffed with vegetables or other fillings such as bamboo shoot, taro or turnip. The puddings are steamed and served (see Stuffed Vegetable Puddings on page 47) but some people prefer fried puddings; so the steamed puddings are pan-fried until the dough is crispy.

4.3. Thai Fried Noodles
Phad Thai   ผัดไทย

Except for the price, this Thai dish makes no difference whether it is served in a cosy restaurant or a hawker stall. It is a favourite for lunch, dinner or even late night supper. Many stalls which exclusively sell Thai fried noodles are so popular that they are crowded most of the time with huge throngs of *phad Thai* lovers.

Going through each visible item in the dish is quite entertaining. The variety of ingredients includes scrambled eggs, beansprouts, dried shrimps, garlic, diced beancurd, minced salted turnip and dry chilli powder. This is a highly-recommended dish which the tourist should not overlook.

4.4. A-la-carte dishes   อาหารตามสั่ง

The basic fact about street cooking is that there is no limit to their invention or creativity. A-la-carte dishes are good examples of this theory. In a show-case, you can see fresh food in such a wide variety that you may not know what the hawker is selling. In this case, just ask and the chance for a 'yes' is high. At this kind of stall where a stove and a wok are the two prominent kitchen utensils, the hawker offers a colourful menu that may include fried rice *khao phad*, fried noodles *kuay-tiao phad,* beef or pork sauteed with chillies noodles *kuay-tiao phad,* beef or pork sauteed with chillies and basil leaves *nua/kai phad kaprao,* sweet and sour vegetables *phad priew wan,* stuffed omelette *khai yad sai,* the famous *tom yam kung* (hot soup with shrimps or other seafood), and many other a-la-carte dishes. We may need one more book to go into more detail, so the most practical way to explore what is available at a food stall where a variety of cook-to-order dishes are offered, is to simply ask the hawker what can be done with this and that and this.

5.1. Spring Rolls
Poh Piah Thod ปอเปี๊ยะทอด

Spring rolls are Chinese snacks known to food enthusiasts world-wide, and Thailand is no exception. Spring rolls can be a snack for the man on the street who simply exchanges a roll for less than a dime and enjoys it while taking a stroll down the street. It is however common to see this snack being served in an expensive Chinese restaurant.

5.2. Fried Wontons
Kiew Thod เกี๊ยวทอด

If you have ever tried Chinese food, chances are you must have tasted and liked wontons, whether in soup or fried. Crispy fried wontons make excellent snacks. History has it that wontons date back to the 13th century when Marco Polo visited China. He reportedly liked the wontons and noodles so much that he took samples back to Italy. Now you know which country inspired the famous ravioli and spaghetti!

5.3. Fried Fish Cakes
Thod Mun Pla   ทอดมันปลา

Most foreign visitors to Thailand like this dish and many never forget to order a dish of *thod mun* whenever they go to a restaurant either in Thailand or in their respective countries. The main ingredients of the dough consist of crushed fresh fish, which is repeatedly pounded until sticky, chilli paste, chopped string beans and fish sauce. The mixed dough is then formed into small round cakes and deep-fried. The fish cakes are served with mixed sauce, cucumber slices, crushed peanuts and vinegar. Fried shrimp cakes or *thod mun kung* are sometimes sold at the same hawker's stall.

5.4. Curry Puffs
Kari-Pub   กะหรี่ปั๊บ

These deep-fried turnovers have the taste and fragrance of curry as the name clearly indicates. Curry paste is an important ingredient of the filling, which has the mixture of diced potatoes, sliced onions, and either minced beef or minced chicken.

5.5. Deep-Fried Locusts
Tuktan Thod   ตั๊กกะแตนทอด

Locusts had never had the 'honour' of becoming food for the Thai until they went on a rampage many years ago, wreaking havoc on farmers' plantations and cornfields. Though deep-fried locusts are now a common hawker food and despite nutritionists' assurances that they are nutritious, many Thais still cannot take to the idea of taking them into the mouth.

Nor can you, probably!

5.6. Fried Toast with Ground Pork/Shrimp
Khanom Pung Na Moo/Kung
ขนมปังหน้าหมู/กุ้ง

A dish familiar among some Asians, this snack is sometimes served during afternoon tea, or as an hors d'oeuvre for lunch or dinner. Ground pork or shrimp mixture is spread on one side of a bread slice, which is later cut into four square pieces and deep-fried. Ground shrimp toasts are also dipped in sesame seeds before being fried. They are served with a sauce mixture of cucumber slices, vinegar and syrup.

This snack is usually sold at a hawker stall together with other deep-fried snacks, for example, fried fish cakes and shrimp cakes.

5.7. Fried Dough Balls
Khanom Khai Hong   ขนมไข่หงษ์

Khanom Khai Hong literally means 'swan egg dessert'. The ball is supposed to be about the size of a swan egg. The dough is fried and sprinkled with sugar.

5.8. Fried Bananas
Kluay Kaek   กล้วยแขก

This dessert is so simple that one can easily identify it at a hawker stall. There are two kinds of fried bananas—one sliced banana dipped in batter and the other a whole banana coated with a mixture of shredded coconut and flour. Sliced potatoes can also be dipped in the same batter and fried, thus making fried potatoes *mun thod*.

5.9. Fried Potato Balls
Khai Nok Kratha   ไข่นกกระทา

Unlike fried potatoes, the potato balls are made of mashed potatoes shaped into balls before they are fried. Fried potato balls are always crispy outside and chewy inside.

5.10. Deep-Fried Dough Sticks
Pa Thong Koh   ปาท่องโก๋

Iew Ja Kuay as it is called in Chinese, the dough sticks are favourite breakfast snacks among Thais and Chinese alike. They are good with coffee as doughnuts are to the Americans or croissants to the French. For those who prefer thick rice soup to coffee for breakfast, the dough sticks can also be cut into small pieces and served with the soup. Taking them with coffee is also superb.

Since *pa thong koh* always consists of two dough sticks attached together, the Thais fondly compare a couple deeply in love and hardly seen separately, to a pair of *pa thong koh*.

5.11 Fried Nuts
Tua Thod   ถั่วทอด

See (page 48, Category 3.9)

6.1. Fried Crabs in Curry Sauce
Pu Phad Pong Kari   ปูผัดผงกระหรี่

A popular dish at seafood stalls or restaurants, cooking this dish is simple and fast. Curry sauce, definitely one of the ingredients, is mixed with soy sauce, chillies (optional) and garlic. The crabs, cut into pieces, are sauteed in the liquid mixture over strong heat.

6.2. Fish Curry Cake in Banana Cups
Ho Mok Pla   ห่อหมกปลา

Banana leaves are common in traditional Thai cooking. Though aluminium foils or plastic bags have made their way into the Thai kitchen in the last few decades, banana leaves remain unchallenged in the art of cooking. This dish is one of the examples where plastic bags can never substitute for banana leaves. The leaves are properly cut and made into cups to contain the fish curry to be steamed.

Major ingredients for the curry cake include fish sauce, coconut milk and fish, which can be replaced with other seafood. This is another delicious favourite dish among local people and foreign visitors.

6.3. Coconut Chicken Curry
Kaeng Kai แกงไก่

Coconut chicken curry is one of the most popular main dishes in every Thai kitchen. Available in expensive restaurants as well as hawker stalls, the curry definitely hot and spicy—is eaten with rice. When beef or fishballs substitute chicken, other ingredients, except for coconut milk which remains, are slightly changed and the taste becomes different.

Beef and fishball curries are known among the Thai as *kaeng nua* and *kaeng luk chin pla* respectively.

6.4. Beef/Chicken Curry with Peanuts
Masaman Nua, Masaman Kai
มัสมั่น เนื้อ/ไก่

Peanuts, hardly used in Thai curries, are added into this dish which is mixed with specially-prepared *masaman* curry paste. Coconut milk, potatoes and onions are cooked in the curry. Though beef is widely added in the curry, chicken also makes an equally tasty dish.

6.5. Pork Rind Soup
Kapoh Pla กระเพาะปลา

Kapoh pla literally means 'fish belly'—the original ingredient of this Chinese dish. Today, pork rind is used instead of the expensive and scarce fish belly but the original name dies hard. The prominent character of stall selling this dish is a large pot inside which the soup is simmering.

The liquid, mixed with cornstarch, is rather thick. Other ingredients include bamboo shoots, soy sauce, bloodcake (most Western people cannot even bear the idea of taking blood!) and chicken.

6.6. Crispy Noodles
Mee Krob   หมี่กรอบ

A favourite hors d'oeuvre widely served in Thai restaurants or buffets, the recipe of this interesting dish is found in nearly every Thai cookbook. This fact can be positively interpreted that the dish is delicious—and it sure is. Rice vermicelli, which are as thin as strands of hair, are fried before they are mixed with seasonings and syrup. Raw beansprouts and green onions are served with the crispy noodles.

6.7. Red Noodles Soaked in Coconut Milk
Mee Kati   หมี่กระทิ

The outstanding character of this dish is rice vermicelli in pink—the result of red food colouring. The dish is a traditional Thai hors d'oeuvre but it is not so popular compared to other noodle dishes.

6.8. Golden Threads, Golden Egg Drops, Golden Egg Cake
Foi Thong, Thong Yip, Thong Yod
ฝอยทอง, ทองหยิบ, ทองหยอด

These desserts are said to have been introduced to Thailand by the Portuguese four centuries ago and have been a favourite in the Thai Royal Court even until today. The man in the street also cannot resist a second bite once he has tried it. Both golden threads and egg cakes are made of egg yolks cooked in boiling syrup. Though the ingredients for the three desserts are similar, the preparation methods are different. For *Foi Thong* or golden threads, the egg batter is let to flow from the tiny hole of a tube into boiling syrup while a spoonful drop of egg batter into the same syrup makes a golden egg ball. For golden egg cakes, the same batter is boiled in the shape of a tiny pancake and later put in a small cup.

6.9. Tapioca Strings in Coconut Syrup
Khanom Plakrim Kai Tao   ขนมปลากิมไข่เต่า

The outstanding character of this dessert is a hawker carrying two baskets each of which has a clay pot. Inside the clay pots are the tapioca strings with two different tastes— one sweet and one a little salty. When served, the two are combined in a bowl.

6.10. Sticky Rice with Different Toppings
Khao Niew Moon   ข้าวเหนียวมูล

Sticky rice, a favourite Thai dessert, can be prepared in so many different ways. This one, glutinous rice cooked with coconut milk, is just one of the many inventions in the Thai kitchen. With sticky rice as the base, the creation of toppings is again not limited to just one. There is a wide variety of toppings including custard _sangkaya_, crushed dried fish _pla haeng_, shredded coconut _kracheek_, ripe mangoes _ma-muang_ and durian in coconut syrup _narm krathi thurian_.

6.11. Boiled Banana in Coconut Syrup
Kluay Buad Chee   กล้วยบวดชี

The bananas mostly used in Thai food and desserts are from a local species called _kluay narm wa_. For this dish, _kluay narm wa_ is cooked in a mixture of coconut milk and sugar. Many hawkers put several aluminium pots on their stalls, so it is rather hard to know what they are selling. This dessert can possibly be inside one of the pots. _Kluay buad chee_ is tasty and worth trying a few bites but don't miss the chance to explore desserts in other pots. After a brief survey, you will be surprised at the huge array of Thai desserts.

6.12. Flower-Shaped Cookies
Khanom Dok Lamduan ขนมดอกลำดวน

This Thai cookie is made in the shape of *Dok Lamduan*, a traditional Thai flower. This cookie tastes very much like Western cookies and the baking method is exactly the same as the Western way of baking. Instead of butter as required in most Western recipes, cooking oil is used for the dough which also has a mixture of flour and sugar.

6.13. Desserts on the Wheel
Rod Khen/Khanom Waan รถเข็นขนมหวาน

As dark falls and the traffic is lighter, a young man would get onto the saddle of his three-wheeler to peddle Thai desserts. This, however, does not mean that Thai people love to take desserts at night. It's only that the vendor who chooses this mode of vending finds it more convenient to move on the city's streets after the afternoon rush hours. In some small lanes or housing estates, these three-wheelers can be seen during daytime. Inside the brightly-lit showcase on the wheel, in case it moves at dusk, are a wide selection of colourful Thai desserts, such as layer cake *khanom chan*, golden threads, golden egg drops and golden egg cakes *foi thong, thong yip, thong yod*, coconut jelly *wun kati*, coconut pudding *sangkaya*, etc. Some vendors add Western pastries and cakes to the showcase.

6.14. Fried Rice with Shrimp Paste
Khao Kluk Kapi   ข้าวคลุกกะปิ

Shrimp paste *kapi*, one of the Thais' favourite ingredients, is mixed in many different dishes. Its strong smell can be unbearable for the Westerner but the local simply cannot do without it for it is the heart of Thai cooking. This particular dish of fried rice is usually topped with thin slices of omelette, dried shrimps, sliced red onions, cooked sweet pork and lemon quarters.

7

ICE-COOLED WAY

7.1. Chestnuts in Syrup
Tub Tim Krob ทับทิมกรอบ

This dessert, always mixed with crushed ice, is appropriate for a warm country like Thailand. After a meal of hot and spicy Thai food, a bowl of this dessert can somewhat 'cure' the burning tongue. In preparing it, water chestnuts are diced and rolled over red-coloured flour before they are boiled in hot water which makes them appear like rubies. The 'rubies' are always mixed with syrup, coconut milk and crushed ice when served.

7.2. Crushed Iced Sweets
Narm Kaeng Sai น้ำแข็งใส

Crushed ice sweets are somewhat equivalent to ice cream of the West. For this dessert, you can select from a wide variety of preserved fruits, including water chestnuts, red beans, lotus seeds, sweetened Chinese red dates, etc., or many other specially-prepared tidbits, each of which is displayed in a bowl. Just point at one or a few kinds of sweet that you like. The sweets are topped with syrup and then crushed ice.

7.3. Black Jelly
Chao Kuay   เฉาก๊วย

Chao kuay is made from a plant of the same name which originated in China. Dried stalks of *chao kuay* are boiled with water for a few hours until the liquid turns black. Cornstarch is then dissolved in the liquid and it becomes jelly cake. Black jelly is usually diced or scratched into long strips before being added with syrup and crushed ice when served. The Chinese believe that *chao kuay* is good in reducing heat in a person's body.

7.4. Sugar-Cane Juice
Narm Oy   น้ำอ้อย

A sugarcane squeezing machine is prominent at a hawker stall selling this beverage. Sugarcanes are freshly squeezed and kept in bottles. Once a customer orders a glass of sugarcane juice, the hawker simply pours it into a glass of ice. It's simple and delicious.

7.5. Longan Juice
Narm Lamyai   น้ำลำใย

Dried longans, or *lamyai* in Thai, are cooked with boiling water which eventually has the flavour of the fruit. Longan juice is usually brown — the colour of dried longans. It is always mixed with crushed ice when served.

7.6. Fruit Juice
Nam Pol-mai น้ำผลไม้

A stall or cart, colourfully decorated with a variety of tropical fruits, is at nearly every corner of Bangkok's sidewalk where hawker stalls are allowed to be erected. Fruit juice is refreshing particularly in a warm climate like Thailand. A hawker also has a blender to blend the fruit juice with crushed ice, so tell the hawker you simply want the juice on the rocks if you don't want it blended. The most common fruits available are oranges, watermelons, bananas, pineapples, coconuts and lemons.

7.7. Local Ice Cream ไอศครีม

When you take ice cream on the sidewalk, don't expect it to taste like or be as creamy as the Western ice cream. Apart from the usual chocolate, vanilla and strawberry ice creams, some hawkers also offer coconut ice cream. Together with any ice cream you choose, you can also ask for toppings, which are mostly made from preserved fruits: red beans, lotus seeds, diced potatoes or tapioca and peanuts. Ice cream hawkers prefer peddling on three-wheelers or some simply go on foot with their push carts.

7.8. Singapore's Green Strings
Lod Chong Singapore ลอดช่องสิงคโปร์

This cooled dessert, said to have originated in Singapore, is a favourite among the Thai especially on a warm day. Some people may have it as an after-meal dessert while others may simply drop in at a hawker stall and order a glass of *Lod Chong Singapore* as a snack. The green strings are made of a dough of crushed green beans mixed with tapioca flour, then boiled. The cooked strings are added with a mixture of coconut juice, water and syrup. Cracked ice is added when served.

7.9. Lotus Root Water
Narm Rak Bua   น้ำรากบัว

This beverage is an excellent refresher and the Chinese, who have introduced lotus roots to the Thai kitchen, believe that lotus root is a kind of herbal medicine that helps cool the body's heat and mild fever. It is not so easy to find a hawker stall selling lotus root water, but if you happen to visit Chinatown, you may find one. Inside the bowl of water, a hawker also puts slices of lotus roots which are also edible.

In addition to a beverage, lotus roots can also be cooked as a main dish, for example, lotus roots and pork rib soup.

7.10. Green Leaf Water
Narm Bai Buabok   น้ำใบบัวบก

Buabok, literally meaning land lotus leaf, is a local plant grown on soil. Its leaf, which appears like a miniature lotus leaf, goes well with some Thai dishes. *Buabok*, boiled with water, gives a beverage unique smell and taste. The water is a good herbal medicine. This green beverage is always at a hawker stall with several other beverages such as lotus root water *narm rak bua*, longan juice *narm lamyai*, white raisin juice *narm luke ked* and lemon juice *narm manao*.

7.11. Chinese Herbal Water
Narm Jub Liang   น้ำจับเลี้ยง

Jub Liang, a Chinese word, literally means the 'ten cool-ness'. The secret of this beverage, which can mostly be found at Chinatown, is the mixture of 10 herbal medicines boiled together. The water from the 10 herbs is believed to be a good natural medicine to cool the body's heat.

8
KEEPING
IT
WARM

8.1. Bean Milk
Narm Tao Hoo   น้ำเต้าฮู้

Bean milk, the juice of yellow mung beans, is a good beverage for breakfast. Most people like to add a little sugar in the hot bean milk. At a hawker stall which sells bean milk, one will also find bowls of different snack items, including tapioca balls, lotus seeds, beancurd sheets which one can choose to put in the bean milk. Bean milk is usually served hot.

8.2. Bird's Nest Soup
Rung Nok   รังนก

Chinese people believe that swallow's nests, made with the bird's saliva, are nutritious and good to a person's health though there has not been any medical theory to substantiate this so far. In Thailand, some private companies have been granted concessions to collect swallow's nests from mountains on islands in the southern part of the country, mostly in the Andaman Sea. The nest collection process is rather painstaking and this explains why the prices of bird's nests are expensive, depending on their quality. A bird's nest is cleaned and soaked for several hours, or overnight, before it is cooked into soup. The price of a bowl of bird's nest soup can fetch up to US$10-20 if the quality of the nest is good (up to human standard), and expensive bird's nest soup is mostly served in Chinese restaurants. The bird's nest soup which you see at a sidewalk stall is said to be mixed with other materials that look like bird's nest, dried and transparent jelly for instance.

8.3. Gingko Nut Soup
  Pae Kuay   แปะก๊วย

In Thailand, gingko nuts are mostly imported from China and it is the Chinese who have introduced these nuts to the Thai. Cooking a bowl of this soup is simple: shell gingko nuts, cook them with water. When served, add a little sugar into the gingko nuts and boiling water. Simple as it is, the price of a bowl of gingko nut soup is, on the other hand, rather expensive because the nuts are not locally grown. If you like it cool, ask the hawker if he has crushed ice.

9
SPECIAL CATEGORY

9.1. Boiled Cockles
Hoy Kraeng Luck หอยแครงลวก

The sight of blood soaked in the cockles, though cooked, may deter even an adventurous taste-bud. For a visitor who has never had this food, it is recommended that he tries only a few bites to first ensure that there is no negative reaction to the digestive system. Cockles or blood clams can be boiled or grilled but most people prefer to have them boiled for the meat is more tender. It is important that the cooked cockles are served with sauces of chillies mixed with minced garlic, vinegar and fish sauce. Cockles are available at most seafood stalls or restaurants.

9.2. Hot and Spicy Salads
Yum ยำ

The nearest English version to *yum* is salad, but chillies, which have no place in Western salads, are almost inevitable in Thai-style salads. Hot and spicy salads are not restricted only to vegetables. They can vary and go as far as a chef — a hawker in this case — can imagine and the names change in accordance with the ingredients, for instance, *'yum nua'* for beef salad, *'yum wun sen'* for vermicelli salad, *'yum yai'* for mixed vegetable salad, *'yum pla muek'* for cuttlefish salad and *'yum ma-muang'* for mango salad. It is rather difficult to know if a hawker is selling hot and spicy salads if you simply look at the stall and are not familiar with the Thai ingredients. You can ask anyway, if you are curious and want to try to see if they are really hot and spicy.

9.3. Thai Noodles with Fish Curry Sauce
Khanom Chine Narm Ya   ขนมจีนน้ำยา

Highlights of this dish are a variety of vegetables and beansprouts, from which one can choose to eat alongside the spicy fish curry sauce. The sauce is composed of boiled and finely-crushed fish, herb and spices. The rice noodles are round like spaghetti, but instead of long strands, the rice noodles are rolled into pieces.

The fish curry sauce, which is always simmered in a large pot (fishballs are sometimes put in the bowl), is poured over the noodles when served. Some people do not find hot and spicy food their cup of tea for breakfast, but many Thais love this dish just before they start their day, or end their evening.

9.4. Crispy Coconut and Tidbits
Miang Khum   เมี่ยงคำ

The fun part of enjoying this snack is to help yourself by taking a little of everything onto a lettuce leaf, topped with sweet sauce of syrup and minced peanuts. The highlight of this snack are coconut flakes made from finely-sliced coconut and roasted over low heat until crispy. Other tidbits are arranged separately on a tray so that one can pick every item and put it onto the lettuce leaf. The tidbits include diced ginger, lemons, red onions, chillies, dried shrimps and roasted peanuts. Most hawkers separately pack every item of the tidbits, the coconut flakes and the syrup sauce in small plastic bags so that one can later arrange them on a tray. At some stalls where tables and chairs, or just a mat, are availabe for customers to sit down, hawkers may arrange these tidbits in a tray for them.

9.5. Fresh Fruits
Pol Mai Sod ผลไม้สด

In fact, it is unnecessary to explain even to a new visitor to Thailand on how to identify a fresh fruit hawker. The fruits inside his pushcart, which can be clearly seen, mostly include pineapple *supparod*, payaya *mala-kaw*, watermelon *taeng-mo*, mango *ma muang*, guava *farang* and rose apple *shomphou*. The fruits are always sold by the piece, and not by weight.

9.6. Preserved Fruits
Pol Mai Dong ผลไม้ดอง

Preserved fruits of different kinds are mostly sold by weight. Some hawkers pack and sell them in plastic bags. A good variety is preserved as dried fruits or food.

9.7. Thai Cookies
Khanom Ping ขนมผิง

Thai cookies are abundant and this dome-shaped biscuit is just one of them. Hawkers always pack them in plastic bags to keep them crispy. The cookies are a little sweet.

9.8. Chinese Cakes with Fillings
   Khanom Piah   ขนมเปี๊ยะ

A Chinese television series once showed the story of a young and who finally became a wealthy busines-man from selling *khanom piah*. In Thailand, there are many Chinese immigrants who are financially successful just from making and selling *khanom piah*. These Chinese cakes are more than simple dessert. They are favourite gifts for various occasions such as weddings and birthdays. The fillings include crushed green mung beans and red beans.

9.9. Sweet Silk Threads with Flour Pancakes
   Roti Sai Mai   โรตีสายไหม

The silk threads are made purely from sugar, so they are no doubt sweet. At a hawker's stall, the sweet silk threads and flour pancakes are always packed in two separate plastic bags. When served, the sweet silk threads are placed on a piece of flour pancake which is rolled over them.

9.10. Bananas in Syrup
   Kluay Chuam   กล้วยเชื่อม

This a dessert purely for the sweet tooth. They are very sweet of course. Bananas are put in boiling syrup and let to absorb the sweetness for several minutes before they are taken out of the pan. When served, the syrup-soaked bananas are topped with coconut cream.

9.11. Tapico Balls in Coconut Syrup
   Bua Loy   บัวลอย

Bua loy literally means floating lotus seeds, but no lotus seed is in the ingredients of this dessert. The reason it is called lotus seed is because of the shape of the taopica balls. Sticky rice flour is added with water and kneaded until still before it is formed in balls about the size of lotus seeds.

The balls are then tossed into a pan of boiling water, after which they float on the surface when cooked. The balls are drained and mixed in coconut milk and sugar.

9.12. Mock Miniature Fruits
Luk Chub   ลูกชุบ

They appear like marzipan of the West but the ingredients and preparation method are different. For this lovely dessert, beans are boiled and crushed until they can be formed in the shapes of tiny fruits. The shaped beans are then painted in the colour of those fruits and dipped in jelly so that they are shiny.

9.13. Bean-filled Crescents
Khanom Tua Paeb   ขนมถั่วแปบ

Glutinous rice is required in a lot of Thai dishes, and so is glutinous rice flour which is prepared in many ways in Thai desserts. It is the glutinous rice flour that makes the dough soft and chewy. The dough is filled with boiled green beans, rolled over shredded coconut, and sprinkled with sugar.

9.14. Chewy Strings
Khanom Niew   ขนมเหนียว

'*Khanom niew*' literally means chewy dessert. Glutinous rice flour plays an important role in giving this dessert its unique character. The dough is prepared almost the same as crescent dough (above) and these two desserts are mostly sold together at a stall or a Thai dessert shop. *Khanom niew* is topped with crispy rice and syrup when served.

9.15. Crispy Rolls
Thong Muan   ทองม้วน

The rolls look like crepes of the West but the batter, when baked, is crispy. In baking a crispy roll, the batter is sandwiched between two flat iron sheets and baked in a charcoal oven. The baked batter is then taken out and rolled into finger size rolls.

9.16. Coconut pudding in Banana Leaf cups
Tako   ตะโก้

Making a cup of banana is as fascinating as preparing this
dessert. The pudding has two layers — the bottom slightly
sweet and the top a little salty. The trick to enjoy the taste
of this dessert is to take the two layers together, never
separately, in one bite. The bottom layer, which is transparent, has the mixture of cornstarch, rice flour, sugar and water
chestnuts or lotus seeds. The top layer has coconut milk as
the main ingredient.

9.17. Layer Cake
Khanom Chan   ขนมชั้น

The art of preparing this dessert is to make each layer of
batter as thin as possible, and to make a cake of as many
layers as possible. Each thin layer of batter which has a
mixture of, among others, rice flour, sugar and coconut milk
is poured into a pan and steamed. A layer is steamed for
about 5-6 minutes before the next one is poured over it, then
steamed again. The same process goes on and on until the
final layer, about the tenth, is finished.

9.18. Boiled Rice with Delicacies
Khaotom Kui   ข้าวต้มกุย

A big bowl of boiled rice is the highlight of this stall where
many other delicacies, already cooked or cooked to order,
are available. Boiled rice stalls are mostly seen on the
pavement in the evening.

HEADING TO THE AREAS

Best eating times

As almost every road is a hawker street, a visitor should have no problem in identifying around a half dozen items in each place at peak time. Areas are star-graded for place popularity and food availability. Many hawkers appear after office hours, around 6.00 pm onwards. Definitely by 7.30 pm, what in the day time had been barren road would have turned into a bright glutton's strip or square. The best time to sample hawkers' food in many places is thus after sunset. Next best time is before lunch, around 10.30 am.

Hawker food can take several hours of simmering for meat to be tender and soup to be saturated with the goodies from bones and ingredients. One good point is that the cooking will not be super-duper microwave quick.

An essential tactical manoeuver

It is better to approach the hawker, place an order first and then sit down, than to wait at a table for some server to come by and take your order. This can be extremely frustrating especially when you have experienced fast, efficient and courteous table-waiting in other countries. Here, at hawker level, don't take this for granted. Have you ever tried waiting 'forever'?

Area arrangements

The areas described below appear in order of convenience for temporary tourists, new residents and all those who itch to taste new things.

'Convenience' means a little English from some vendors may be expected, there could be chairs to sit without too much waiting and the area is cleaner and looks more appealing for a food environment.

1. Silom/Surawong Roads Area ✦✦✦

Bus services : ***(Bold print means air-conned)***
Silom : **2, 5, 4, 27**. 15, 50,76, 77, 115,
Surawong : 1, 16, 35, 36, 93, 112.
Key roads : Silom/ Surawong Roads.
Area landmarks : Dusit, Montien, Tawana Ramada,
Holiday Inn, Narai, hotels.
Robinson, Central, Dept. Stores.
Bestt ime : 6.30 pm onwardsnear Patpong;
lunch hour, 11.00 am onwards
near Central Department Store.

This is the 'Wall Street' region of Bangkok, a sophisticated busy business area. There are many hawkers towards evening when nearby Patpong, the city's freewheeling night spot, awakens.

Silom, meaning 'windmill,' is also a tourist area frequented by well-heeled Thais and foreign residents.

1 - Silom /Surawong Roads Area

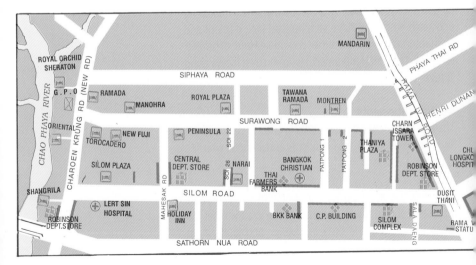

Most popular is a take-away order as sitting space is crammed in this bus y square, but one can also find a seat at many of the stalls located just after Robinson Department Store. Fried, toasted or roasted meaty chunks are the order of the day.

Due to the numerous offices, lunch-time meals can be exciting. Look for hawkers in the lanes, not on Silom or Surawong Road themselves. There's chicken rice, beef noodles, ready-cooked dishes and lots of other exciting dishes to discover. Search around the Central Department Store area from Soi 20-26; you will bump into something 'nice-looking' and deliciously tempting.

At Lumpini Park, at the main entrance under very shady trees, in the weekend evenings you can treat yourself to sitting on little stools or squating down on the turf for food that includes *Isaan som-tam* or papaya salad, barbecued meat, roasted eggs and sweet potatoes, iced drinks and local candies and confectioneries.

Some Westerners have not even tried steamed peanuts while sitting on a bench in the park or in front of a department store. Why not? *(See what the doctor says about nuts at the end of the book.)* Locals take steamed peanuts the way Americans eat popcorn.

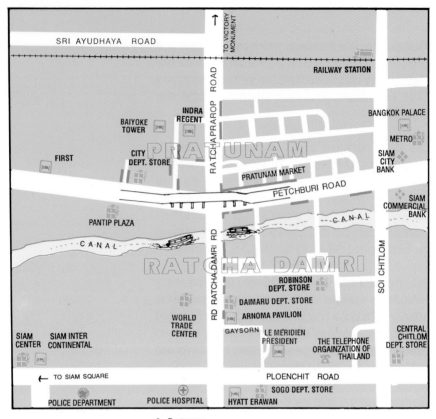

2 - Pratunam

2. Pratunam ✦✦✦

Bus services : **4, 5, 11, 12, 13, 14,** 2, 11, 13, 14, 17, 23, 38, 45, 54, 60, 74, 77, 79, 93, 99, 204.

Key roads : Petchburi, Ratchaprarop, Phayathai.

Area landmarks : Bayoke Tower/Indra Regent, First, Asia hotels. World Trade Center.

Best time : Depends on specific places of the area, but lunch or dinner time is best.

Pratunam means 'water gate' but whatever water there had been is today paved over with asphalt and overrun by hawkers.

The parabolic metal fencing on the right corner of the junction if you face towards the Indra Shopping Complex at the flyover, is where at least two dozen hawkers cram together to compete in eatery vendoring. This place is very popular with locals and so far, only a few Caucasians, generally ladies.

Here, one can experience restaurant menu-type dishes not so commonly found elsewhere. There are the deep-fried prawns, steamed crabs, fried oysters with egg and other 'uncommon' dishes for a hawker. This is the best site though there are other stalls near the pedestrian bridge along the lanes selling more usual hawker foods.

One can enjoy a full meal with desserts and tidbits without moving from the chair but prices tend to be on the higher side.

If a short walk is taken along Petchburi Road away from Bata Shoe shop near the overpass, there is a line of vendors with their own interesting specials. This is actually a continuation from the corner.

In the evening, opposite this stretch where a Thai cinema is located, there are numerous stalls that offer a wide range of heavy-type meals and noodles. Well-dressed office girls and better-dressed cinema-going ladies sit and slurp side by side.

Where Robinson Department Store almost crashes into Daimaru Department Store, stalls make use of the lanes to serve lunch hunters.

Opposite and around the First Hotel and similarly about the Asia Hotel at Phayathai Road is another good hunting area. Where office buildings have closed for the day, hawkers open up for the night selling mainly noodles, a couple with *yen tao fo*. เย็นตาโฟ

3. Banglumpoo ✦✦✦

Bus services : **2, 11.** 3, 6, 9,
19, 30, 31, 32, 33, 34, 56.
Key roads : Chakaphong / Khao San.
Area landmarks : The Democracy Monument,
Vieng Tai Hotel;
Merry King, Central, Department
Stores.
Best time : 10.00 am to 6.00 pm.
No good after 7.00 pm

This area has two distinct features: one, it has very-well stocked shops of cheaper but yet good quality ladies' clothing and stacks of jeans, T-shirts and costume jewellery. There is the 8-storey New World Department Store surrounded by lesser but also impressive stores.

It is also the most popular haunt for budget travellers. There are guest houses, coffee houses, eating shops, travel

3 - Banglumpoo

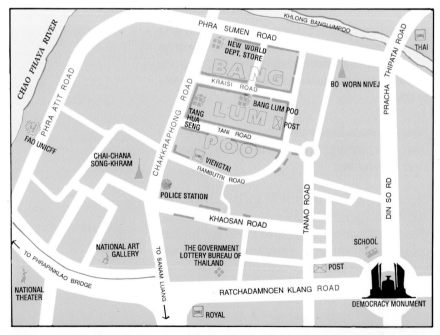

agents, tour operators, second-hand bookshops, cassette tape vendors, handicraft dealers and other vendors. The key road is Khao San.

Within this popular vicinity, hawkers line every available space on the walkways, along the streets, in the alleys and at junctions. Walking is often shoulder-to-shoulder tight in the late afternoons.

One welcoming sight is that almost every hawker seems to be 'just starting business' as there is a high demand for hawker food in this area.

In great variety are local confectionery items in neat plastic-wrapped packages, crispy fried nuts and iced drinks like sugar cane water, coconut water and fresh orange juice.

The 'heavies' include pork leg rice, noodles, Chinese noodle, chicken/roast pork rice and fried meat/fish balls. Some of the stalls work closely with adjacent eating shops so that you can sit inside the shop in comfort and have the hawker bring the food in.

A note: Those shops obviously catering for foreign visitors would prepare Thai dishes in the 'European way'. Try Fried Rice and you will see the difference.

All taxis and tuk tuks know the area.

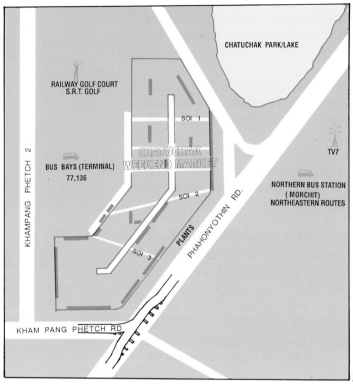

4 - Chatuchak

4. Chatuchak ♦♦♦

Bus services	: **2,3,9,10,29**.8,26,27
	29, 34, 38, 39, 59, 63, 96.
Key road	: Phahonyothin Road.
Area landmarks	: Morchit Bus Terminal for North
	& Northeastern Routes.
Best time	: 9.00 am to 5.00 pm.

This Weekend Market, opening from around 6.00 am till 6.30 pm on Saturdays and Sundays has some authentic Northern and Northeastern foodstalls.

An easily noticeable beef noodle stall is a wooden boat with a long bow bedecked with garlands. It is a stall shaped like a boat.

Or is it a boat turned into a stall? Whatever, this boat-stall is the actual cooking place.

Many such 'boaters' sell the same thing at different sites all over the market. They sell beefball noodles basically with the noodles coming in different sizes of thickness. Many are able to prepare spicy ground beef that goes well with beer, if you drink this funny liquid.

There are stalls inside the market proper as well as around the perimeter. The stalls inside the market are 'heavy meal' types while those along the perimeter are more on barbecued delicacies like deep-fried locusts, small whole birds, chicken thighs, meat balls.

Lighter snacks are steamed nuts, steamed corn, cakes, toasted coconuts and 'cooling' drinks like sugar-cane water, Chinese chestnut water and seaweed drinks, all standing side by side, aerated. Sometimes there are three or four carts selling exactly the same thing next to each other.

For stall drinks, you are bound to come across whole young coconuts burnt blacker than charcoal or sugar-cane juice.
> *Note: you may also want to try pure cane juice, that is, undiluted with neither plain water nor sugar added.*

Near the bus bays for service 77, 136 and others, a woman sits on a stool and fries prawn crackers, peanuts in corn-starch flakes and other nuts. The prawn crackers are a hit with many visitors.

5. Soi Tonglo ✦✦✦

Bus services	:	**13,1, 12,** 25, 38, 40, 48, 98.
Key roads	:	Sukhumvit Soi 55.
Area landmarks	:	Science Museum & Planetarium.
Best time	:	11.00 am to 10.00 pm.

This lane, Soi 55, off Sukhumvit, has a number of hawkers who understand English, as deeper into the soi are residential houses and upper-class apartments.

Many hawkers are out in the evening, especially around the bus station, Ekamai, and stretched out along Sukhumvit Road itself.

Most of the roadside food that stretches into the late evening would be actually from shops that make use of the pavement for chairs and tables. These outlast itinerant vendors who close earlier, around 9.00 pm.

Along Tonglo itself, one may like to buy a roast chicken that is being grilled in front of the onlooker or order a bowl of noodles from the many stalls around.

One noticeable feature is the number of fruit stalls selling local and imported fruits at the junction of Sukhumvit Road.

5 - Soi Tonglo

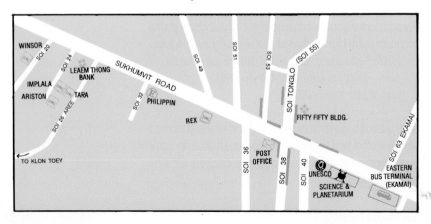

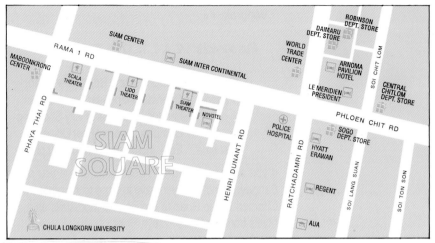

6 - Siam Square: Ploenchit Road

6. Siam Square: ✦✦ Ploenchit Road

    Bus services : **1, 8,** 15, 25, 40, 48, 73,
                   106, 204.
     Key roads : Rama I/Phayathai.
 Area landmarks : Siam Intercontinental,
                   Novotel, hotels.
                   Mah Boon Krong shopping arcade.
     Best time : 10.00 am to 9.00 pm

This is a 'young couples' area basically due to three cinemas located close by and the resultant junk food outlets which are numerous with almost all names represented.

Hawker stalls are mainly located outside the cinemas with some in various lanes within the square. A problem here is sitting. Most hawkers have no tables or chairs as many 'take home' to the movie halls or sit on flower bed railings. On sale are barbecued squid, meatballs, liver chunks, sometimes satay, leaf- wrapped snacks.

Particularly saturated is the short stretch near the pedestrian bridge towards Mah Boon Krong building.

7. Bangrak. ✦✦

Bus services : **2, 4,** 1, 15,17,35,75, 76,
77, 115.
Key road : Charoen Krung Rd(or New Road).
Area landmarks : Oriental, Shangri-la, Royal Orchid
Sheraton hotels, River City Shopping
Complex. General Post Office
Best time : Early morning and from 6.00 pm.

If you are around any of these hotels above you are in Bangrak district. But you have to cross to the other side of Charoen Krung Road to find hawker food-stalls as these hotels front the Chao Phraya River.

You don't have to cross anywhere if you are already in one of the following hotels: Ramada, Manohra, New Fuji, Silom Plaza.

7 - Bangrak

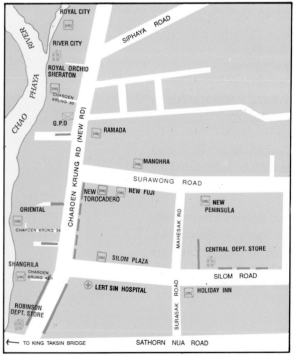

To explore more, walk south towards King Taksin Bridge and quite a few 'Chinese Thai' vendors will be encountered. Ask the hawker if something fascinates you, as the food may be very 'difficult' to find elsewhere.

Bangrak is the tail end of Silom Road towards the Chao Phraya River. Not quite 'hawkers' but placed on walkways in front of some shops are delicious snacks prepared Chinese-style.
Try the glutinous rice in peanuts, with roast pork strips and egg yolk.

Look out for Chinese dumpling—the triangular and leaf—wrapped thing tied with rafia. A couple of shop fronts hawk these.

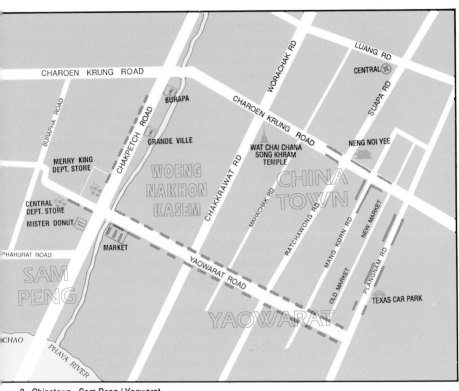

8 - Chinatown - Sam Peng / Yaowarat

8. Chinatown - Sam Peng / Yaowarat ◆◆◆

Bus services : **1, 7, 8**, 1, 4, 11, 25, 35, 53, 73, 75.

Key roads : Charoen Krung, (New Road)/ Yaowarat.

Area landmarks : Goldsmith shops along both these roads. Merry King, Central, Department Stores.

Best time : Lunch and say 7.00 pm till around midnight

The hawker stalls actually occur in the lanes between these two roads, and a few at junctions. Other stalls that cram in to make the place busier are consumer dry-goods like watches and sunglasses, toys and other household items.

Chinatown of course is bigger than just these two roads but here, one does not have to walk too far to get bewildered. The Chinese are natural gluttons be they Thai or what and porridge is a favourite with them, *joak*.

These hawkers - more truly, walkway intruders by shops - stack their cooked bits of fish, meat, and eggs against uncooked vegetables and dried foodstuff, all slanting away on a huge tray with electric bulbs so low one would think eaters are blind. This is the *joak* stall from which many things can be concocted to go with the *joak*.

Along Charoen Krung Road (a very long road) there are numerous push carts at nearly all junctions. Try evening, when other vendors appear to display their non-edible trade as well, making the place lively, attracting hawkers.

A 'unique' item is herbal-medicinal teas/drinks alongside blended fruit juices. The Thai Chinese still maintain their ethnic culture very rigidly despite being Thais, so a visitor can expect things 'more-Chinese' than Thai.

Bird's nest soup is popular as a simple drink after say, dry longevity egg noodles. The Chinese believe that taking semi-boiled cockles is good for revitalising whatever needs revitalising and so this can also easily be seen, the greyish seashells alive and kicking.

Lunch time is a good period to survey some of the many stalls all over Chinatown. If you have located Merry King Department Store, look across the road, where there is a maze of big umbrellas fighting for space with canvas sheets near a bridge. Got it? Head for it.

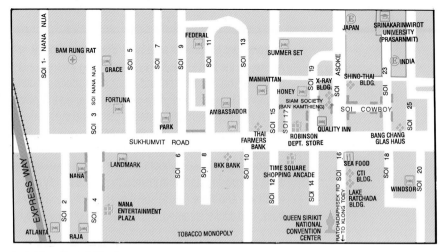

9 - Soi Nana Nua - Soi Cowboy

9. Soi Nana Nua-Soi Cowboy ◆◆◆

Bus services : **1, 8, 11, 13,** 2, 25, 38, 40, 48, 98, 136.
Key roads : Sukhumvit/Soi Cowboy/
Nana Nua/Asoke.
Area landmarks : Nana, Raja, Grace, Park,
Fortuna, hotels at one end;
Ambassador, Manhattan,
Landmark,Somerset,
Honey, hotels at the other end.
Also many inns and guest houses.
Robinson, Times Square Shopping
Arcades
Seafood Restaurant on
Sukhumvit Road.
Best time : 10.00 am, then 7.00 pm
along Sukhumvit.
Soi Asoke : lunch time (10.30-2.00 pm).

This area is a tourist 'walking street', from Soi Nana Nua at the Nana Hotel down to Soi Cowboy, (off Asoke/Soi 23 Sukhumvit). It would take perhaps forty-five minutes of leisurely walking and peeping at store windows here and there. It is not a very long stretch.

A prominent all-hawker area is at Sukhumvit Soi 19, off Asoke, on the turn at the X-Ray Lab building where guests of Honey Inn, Quality Inn and other such modest hotels frequent. The lunch time office crowd has turned this place into a very popular roadside eating place and the hawkers are all lined up under a permanent roof.

There are also those vendors that come and swell up the already crowded stalls with their carts, parked simply on the road here and there. These serve over-the-charcoal items, fruits, iced drinks, steamed maize and other light takeaways.

Along Sukhumvit Road near the Landmark Hotel is a strip well patronised by pedestrian tourists in the evenings. In front of the Thai Farmers' Bank, some stalls sell into the wee hours.

Food ranges from chicken-rice meal dishes through snacks down to ice drinks like iced black coffee. The coffee stall sells bread steamed soft to go with egg custard that many locals find tempting.

At Soi Cowboy, on Soi 23, noodles and grilled meat stalls come out around 7.00 pm and stay till almost midnight, or 10.00 pm sometimes when everything has been sold off.

Soi Cowboy is a scaled down version of Patpong, hence the late hours, hence also no place to sit. If you think you are single, you could order a glass of beer, sit on a road side table and have some hawker food bought by you brought for everybody. 'Everybody' would be the bevy of bar hostesses that appear from thin air when the smell and sight of food materialise. Some of the ladies have very creative versions of hawker food, if you are game; but be warned here and now of a possible financial catastrophe.

This is also one strip where you are likely to see the Indian nuts hawker with a small table on his head. He is always walking. Try a mixture of nuts that are relished with chopped onion shoots and salt for ten baht.

10. Klong Toey ✦✦✦

Bus services	: **7,**22, 45, 46, 109, 115,116,4, 13, 14.
Key roads	: Junction, Ratchadaphisek & Rama IV Roads, Sunthorn Kosa.
Area landmarks	: The Klong Toey Market.
Best time	: 7.00 pm until 10.00 pm.

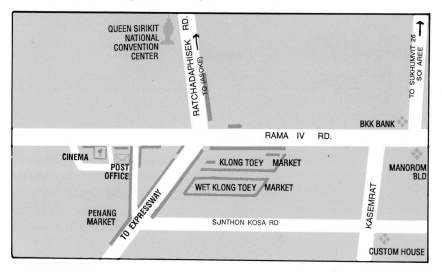

10 - Klong Toey

Some one hundred or more stalls begin to connect motor-car batteries or join other cord extensions to work fluorescent tubes for the evening's business when daytime traffic is gone.

Klong Toey by day is very busy and dirty because of the wet market but by evening, the range of food available makes the area popular with people around the neighbourhood. Everything is steaming hot, the carts fully loaded with their own foodstuffs.

The 'king' of them all is an extremely well-patronised stall of the boiled insides of the pig, namely, giblet soup. The stall is at the left side of the junction of Rama IV and Ratchadaphisek Road if you come down straight from Soi Asoke. It is impossible to miss this stall because of its many tables and the locality. The dish is taken with rice or by itself. This area has a stall selling essence of cobras at a small fortune a cup. Westerners may be repelled at the thought of eating cobra meat but some locals willingly pay as much as 500 baht for a live reptile to be cooked on the spot.

11. Transport Terminals:

❖ Such places are bound to have a few hawkers so long as there are buses coming and going. There are four such areas of reasonable popularity and all of them would have noodles, rice, definitely plastic-wrapped dumplings and snacks of sorts, drinks and biscuits of all shapes.

❖ On sunny weekends, refreshment stalls of coconut, jellies and fruit juices increase in number. Refer to the map for the following locations:

11.1. Hualumpong, Bangkok's Central Railway Station ✦✦

Along the left side as you leave the main door, facing the road are two small lanes, with canopies overshadowing so much that a quick glance is very discouraging, as it reminds one of some dead alley or cul-de-sac.

But ramble on inside and a whole colourful array of stalls and smells unfolds. They look delicious, some say it's worth a go and others say it's expensive. It's a combination of all. Rice and noodles are prepared and sold in many ways.

11.2. Morchit, North/Northeastern Bus Terminal ✦✦

This is a huge complex opposite the Chatuchak Park on Phahonyothin Road. It does not deserve a three-star rating because of the extremely indifferent attitude of many of the sellers, even those of waitresses in air-conditioned places, but there is food variety.

The situation is understandable: this is Bangkok's most crowded terminal. Some semi-permanent stalls (with food brought in by pick-up trucks around 4.00 am in some cases) charge exorbitant prices. It is best to buy from real hawking stalls erected right on the road, blocking even pedestrians.

11.3. Ekamai, The Eastern Bus Terminal ✦✦

This is just before Soi 42, Sukhumvit Road, coming from town. The hawkers here move about a lot because it is a busy transport station and they cause congestion on the roadwalk. There are a few die hards though and one tasty beef noodle stall near the nearest bus-stop is there around 9.00 am until quite late in the evening.

But some worth-the-money stuff is found in the shops. Many were one-time hawkers that gradually moved into shops. Try the chicken rice, pork leg rice and beef noodles, all along the same row, near the green pedestrian overhead bridge.

11.4. The Southern Bus Terminal

Being the newest bus-stand, this place is neat and clean: no hawkers. But there must be, otherwise it is not Thailand!

There are. And they are found before this terminal is reached. As buses tend to depart for long destinations only from around 6.00 pm, hawkers come in around 5.00 pm though a few are around nearly the whole day.

12. Non-Tourist Areas

12.1. Saphan Kwai/Suthisarn ✦✦

Bus services : **2, 3, 5, 10, 13**, 8, 26, 27, 29, 34,38,
39, 54, 63, 74, 77,96, 97, 112, 204.
Key roads : Phahonyothin/Suthisarn/Pradipat.
Area landmarks : Embassy, Liberty, hotels.
Best time : Before and after office hours.

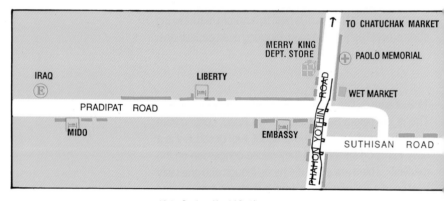

12.1 - Saphan Kwai / Suthisarn

'Saphan Kwai' means 'Buffalo Bridge' but today the only buffaloes visible are those behind steering wheels. This is a crowded area and inconsiderate car drivers and desperate bus handlers make it hard to give a three-star rating, but some food along Suthisarn Road deserves this rating as do some not-so-clean looking but good food stalls near the two hotels on Pradipat Road.

The stalls along Suthisarn Road cater for evening patrons to the strings of bars (not recommended for foreigners unless accompanied by a known friend). In fact, if one is not totally new to Bangkok, one may try this area to buy many 'over the charcoal' snacks.

12.2. Ramkhamhaeng University ✦✦

Bus services	: 1, 12, 14, 126, 58, 60, 71, 92, 93, 95, 109, 113, 115, 207.
Key road	: Ramkhamhaeng Road, Hua Mark.
Area landmarks	: Huamark Stadium/Bus Interchange. Welco, Central, The Mall, Department Stores.
Best time	: 5.30 pm onwards to around 10.00 pm.

Soi 29 in this area offers the most choice in the evening hours. A few other lanes up and down from here have scattered hawker stalls, mostly of take-away ready-cooked food. This is catering for the thousands of university students staying around the place. A good number of not-so-far-away department stores with food centres within have caused hawkers to switch to drinks and snacks.

It is not easy to find the 'heavy meal' type of food with a place to sit for there is simply no place for sitting. All stalls selling dishes-for-rice expect buyers to request for 'take away'.

12.2 - Ramkhamhaeng University

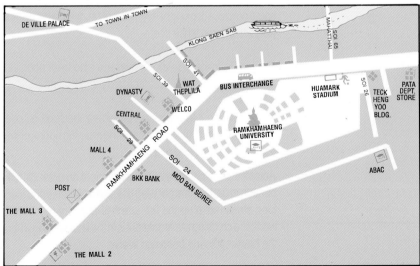

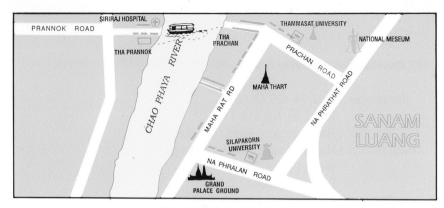

12.3 - Tha Prachan

12.3. *Tha Prachan* ✦✦✦

Bus services : **6, 8, 12.** 25, 31, 51, 30, 39, 44,
59, 201, 80, 91, 203.
Key roads : Na Phrathat/ Na Phralan/Prachan.
Area landmarks : University of Silpakorn,
University of Thammasat,
The Grand Palace, Prachan Pier
(River Boat).
Best time : Lunch hour, from 11.00 am.

The Prachan Pier, where for one baht, you get ferried across the Chao Phraya in five minutes, is a good place to start looking at the cluster of hawker-shops that really have some delicious-looking heavy meals of ready-cooked dishes (to go with plain white rice).

On this Bangkok side of the river are also beef noodles, refreshments, plenty of confectionery and fruits.

Before getting into the pier area where the food is, one passes through a market scene, in the morning hours, of the usual vegetables and seafood.

Across the river, you have to walk straight on upon disembarking to get to some pork-leg rice stalls. Noodles and fried food stuffs make up the list, which is not very much. Not worth the crossing really unless it is in the late evening when the hawking scene becomes livelier.

There are some tasty noodle soup stalls here - beef and pork with the usual smoke smouldering up from roasting meat from many stalls.

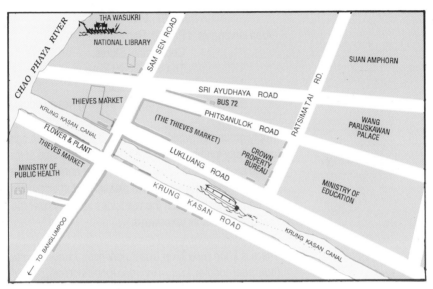

12.4 - Theves

12.4. Theves ✦✦

Bus services : **5, 6** ,3, 19, 30, 31, 32, 33, 53, 55, 64, 65, 90.
Key roads : Sam Seng/Phitsanulok / Lukluang.
Area landmarks : National Library, Ministry of Health.
Best time : Lunch and after office hours.

Four bus route endings just a minute away from the National Library make the junction of Sam Sen/Chakraphong Roads very interesting for hawker food stalls in the evening hours. The area is known for potted plants and flowers and the road to Tha Theves (Theves Pier) has hawkers squatting here and there. Chicken Rice, Fried Oysters, Barbecued Meat, Noodle Soup and Boiled Cockles are around from 10.00 am.

12.5. Victory Monument ✦✦

Bus services : **2, 3, 10, 13, 14**, 8, 26, 27, 28, 29, 34, 38, 39, 54, 59, 63, 74, 75, 77, 96, 97, 112.

Area landmarks : People, Robinson, Department Stores. The monument in the centre of the traffic island.

Best time : whole day but evening has an edge.

Empty ground between roads around the circle has light food all day long but there are a few stalls situated at the bridge area over the canal. This is rather narrow and the canal is unfortunately not quite pleasing. Staff workers of department stores roam the roadsides and buy over-the-charcoal snacks as takeaways.

There is *khao moo krop* (roast pork rice), *kuay-tiao rua* (boat beef noodle), *kuay-tiao moo* (pork noodles), *po piah* (spring rolls) and quite a few other items.

Some hawkers may not stay at one place and they appear only at certain hours of the day, sort of 'time hawkers' if you like.

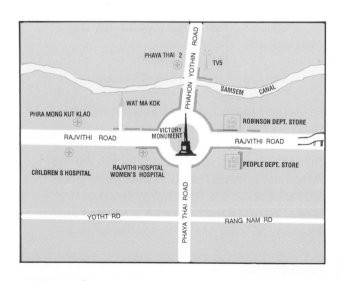

12.5 - Victory Monument

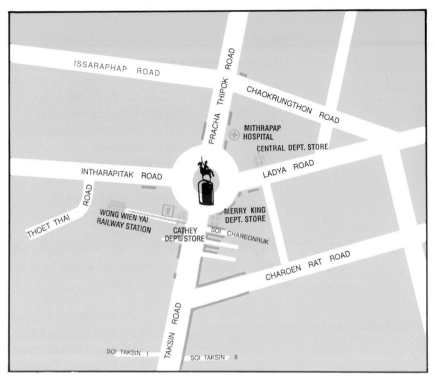

12.6 - Thonburi

12.6. Thonburi ✦✦

```
   Bus services : 6, 10. 3, 6, 7, 9, 20, 43, 84, 105, 111.
    Key roads  : Taksin/Prachatipok.
Area landmarks : Statue of King Taksin,
                 Railway Station,
                 Merry King, Central, Department
                 Stores, Thonburi Hotel.
     Best time : All-day but not consistent.
```

Around this area, in the many sois off the main roads, at the
railway station platform and opposite this, there are sufficient stalls for 'something for eat' when hungry. Near the
wet market, hawkers can be seen from 9am till about 1.00
pm and then around 6.00 pm again but this is only a rough
guide as certain days many seem to have forgotten to
come. It is best to go near the two department stores.

12.7. Phrakhanong ✦✦✦

Bus services	:	**1, 12, 14.** 22, 40, 71, 109, 115.
Key roads	:	Sukhumvit Road, between Soi 71 and 77, Phrakhanong-Klongton Rd (Soi 71 Sukhumvit).
Area landmarks	:	Asian, Welco, ATM, Edison, Daimaru, Department Stores.
Best time	:	Whole day, from 6.00 am near bus stops.

This place, around Sukhumvit Soi 71, is very popular with locals. Hawkers open up business in the early hours and sometimes stretch into the late evening.

12.7 - Phrakhanong

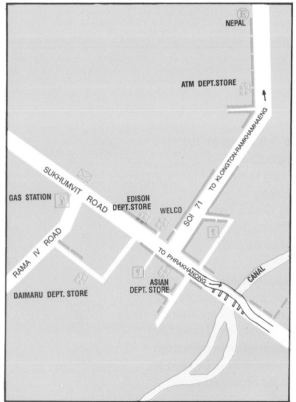

For landmarks, note department stores: Asian, Edison, Welco and ATM and meander in the lanes. These four stores are just about twenty minutes' walk of each other but every two minutes you will encounter stalls.

There are noodles of beef, pork, fish and rice in nearly all servings: duck, pork leg, roast pork, chicken (steamed and roasted), Chinese noodles with fish gravy, *khanom jeen*, is particularly popular. The stalls are mostly on the left if you had come from Sukhumvit Road into Soi 71.

In the evenings, along Soi 71, fried oysters, barbecued

meat, fried noodles, porridge and many more that are absent during daytime are out in full force, complete with fruit stalls, ice-water stalls and other nick nacks within 'shouting distance'. Within 50 metres, one can have a full meal easily.

Another interesting site is behind the row of shop houses fronting the main Sukhumvit Road just before the canal, on the right, upon coming out of Asian Department Store. This is an evening-business-only area and the small but congested square has heavy-meal kind of food: rice-with-this or that-with-rice. The area caters for shop assistants who leave only around 9.30 pm.

SELECTED HAWKER FOOD SITES
AROUND BANGKOK

SAY IT IN THAI

Note: The following hints are taken from 'Practical Thai' by Suraphong Kanchananaga.

Vowels

aa	is pronounced like	'a' in barn
ae	"	`a' in mat or tan
ai	"	`i' in high or fine
ao, au, ow	are "	`ow' in how or down
aw	is "	`aw' in paw or `o' in song
ee	"	`ee' in bee
ei	"	`a' in able or `ai' in air
eu	" somewhat like	'u' in suet
o	" "	`o' in more or vote
oo, ou	are " like	`u' in rule
u	is pronounced like	'oo' in book or 'u' in full

When a vowel is repeated (as in *rawaang*) the effect is to lengthen it to almost double the length of a single vowel. It is very important to keep the distinction between long and short vowels to avoid confusion (e.g: *rawang* means 'to be careful' but *rawaang* means 'middle' or 'between.')

Consonants

b, d, f, k, l,   )
m, p, s, v, w, y) normally, these are pronounced as in
English.

ch   nearly as in church, chat.
sh   as in Shanghai, shell.
d   initial 'd' like in English; final 'd' like 't' in cat.
g   as in gun, but not as in gem or gin.
ng   as in singing, banging.
th   as in aspirant.
ph   as in pony
r   is often nearly silent, as in arm.

Tones

There are five tones:
high (')   middle (no mark)   falling (^)
low (')   rising ( )

Tonal differences can represent a significant difference in
meaning,
e.g: *ma* is dog, but *ma* is horse while *ma* is come.
    ha is five, but *ha* is find.

In speaking Thai, emphasis should be given on the overall
sounds and the rhythm in sentences rather than single
words.

Articles

There is no article in the Thai language. To indicate a
definite object the demonstrative adjectives *ni* (this, these)
and *nanh*(that, those) are used and follow the qualifying
word: the house= *baan nanh*;
this book = *nang sue ni* (or *nangsue lem ni*).

Adjectives

This follows the noun it qualifies:
big fish = *pla yai*; small plate = *chaan lek*.

Verbs

When constructing a sentence, the principal order is subject - verb - object:

I eat rice   = *pom kin khao*
I drink water = *pom duem narm*
He drinks water = *khao duem *narm*

*There is no change in the form of verb to indicate person or number.

krup/ka

'*krup*' often shortened to '*kup*' is used by men after a sentence.
'*ka*' is used by women or girls.

It has no English equivalent but is a polite word to wrap up the sentence. Used by itself, it means 'yes, ok, will do,' e.g:

Are you hungry?= *hew mai krup* (hungry or not?)
yes = *krup*

There is more to grammar and rules than these but remembering these few will help one get by, albeit clumsily but at least communicatively. A couple of repetitions and some gestures will help, for many hawkers have an inkling of what foreigners may not like, such as chilli or blood cakes.

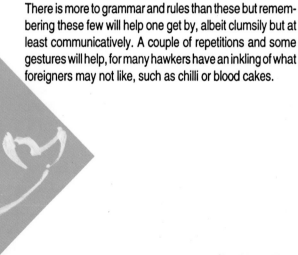

English	Thai	Script
Excuse me, please	*kor thod krup/ka*	ขอโทษครับ/ค่ะ
Thank you (very) much	*korp khun (maak)*	ขอบคุณ (มาก)
This food is delicious	*ahan ni aroy*	อาหารนี่อร่อย
I like it	*pom chop*	ผมชอบ
This is very pungent	*ni phet maak*	นี่เผ็ดมาก
Do you have tissue paper?	*mee kradat tissue mai?*	มีกระดาษทิชชูไหม?
How much is this, please?	*ni thowrai?*	นี่เท่าไหร่?
I am hungry	*pom hue*	ผมหิว
I am thirsty	*pom hue nam*	ผมหิวน้ำ

English	Thai		Script
Do you have fried rice?	*mee khao phad mai?*		มีข้าวผัดไหม?
Do you have plain water?	*mee narm plao mai?*	you can add the word *Krup*	มีน้ำเปล่าไหม?
Do you have iced water?	*mee narm khaeng plao mai?*		มีน้ำแข็งเปล่าไหม?
Do you have hot/iced coffee?	*mee kafe ron/ yenmai?*		มีกาแฟร้อน/เย็น ไหม?
Do you have cigarettes?	*mee buri mai?*		มีบุหรี่ไหม?

English	Thai	Script
Please bring me	*-karuna aow (or: khor)*	กรุณาเอา (หรือ : ขอ)
-whisky and soda	*-Mekhong lae soda*	แม่โขงและโซดา
-fried rice with pork	*-khao phad moo*	ข้าวผัดหมู
-a plate of plain rice	*-khao plao nueng chaan*	ข้าวเปล่าหนึ่งจาน
-fork and spoon	*-shonn-somm*	ช้อน,ส้อม
-salt and pepper	*-kleua lae phrik thai*	เกลือและพริกไทย
-an ash tray	*-thi-khia buri*	ที่เขี่ยบุหรี่
-some toothpicks	*-mai chim faahn*	ไม้จิ้มฟัน
-another glass of iced coffee	*-kafe yen ik kaew*	กาแฟเย็นอีกแก้ว
-another bottle (of beer)	*-bier ik kuat nueng*	เบียร์อีกขวดหนึ่ง
-hot water/tea (Chinese)	*-nam ron/cha ron*	น้ำร้อนชาร้อน
-my bill (take money now)	*-kep tung*	เก็บตังค์

English	Thai	Script
Pack this up for me (to take home)	-ni sai tung	นี่ใส่ถุง
Please give me another plastic bag	-kor tung plastik ik	ขอถุงพลาสติกอีก
I want two/three packets, please	-tongkang sorng- sam bai	ต้องการ 2-3 ใบ
I'm eating here	-pom kin thini	ผมจะกินที่นี่
May I sit here/there?	-nahng thini/thinon dai mai?	นั่งที่นี่/ที่โน่นได้ไหม?
May I share this table with you?	-nahng duay dai mai krup?	นั่งด้วยได้ไหมครับ
Keep the change	-mai thong thorn	ไม่ต้องทอน
I shall be back again	-pom cha ma ik	ผมจะมาอีก

English	Thai	Script	English	Thai	Script
chilli	phrik	พริก	I like it spicy	chorp phet	ชอบเผ็ด
garlic	kra thiam	กระเทียม	is it ready yet?	set yang	เสร็จยัง
onion	hua hawm	หัวหอม	what's this?	ni arai	นี่อะไร
pepper	phrik thai	พริกไทย	not enough	mai phor	ไม่พอ
salt	kleua	เกลือ	put (some) salt	sai kleua	ใส่เกลือ
sugar	narm taan	น้ำตาล	too much	mak pai	มากไป
oil	narm man	น้ำมัน	it is very cold	nee yen mak	นี่เย็นมาก
fish sauce	narm pla	น้ำปลา	no eggs please	mai sai kai	ไม่ใส่ไข่
soy sauce	si yu	ซีอิ๊ว	prawns are fresh	kung sod	กุ้งสด
lime	manao	มะนาว	fish is smelly	pla men	ปลาเหม็น
vinegar	narm som sai choo	น้ำส้มสายชู	this is not fresh	ni mai sod	นี่ไม่สด
meat balls	luk-chin	ลูกชิ้น	make special	tham piset	ทำพิเศษ
vegetable	phak	ผัก	normal	thamada	ธรรมดา
big/small	yai/lek	ใหญ่/เล็ก	goodbye	lar korn	ลาก่อน

WHAT THE DOCTOR SAYS
(...and grandma declared)

1. For a good digestion, we should eat our food slowly chewing it well. (Also to enjoy the cooking.)

2. It is most unwise to swim immediately after a heavy meal.

3. Fruit skins are good sources of vitamins. We should eat what can be eaten, after a thorough washing.

4. What a monkey can eat, we humans can safely follow.

5. Plain water is the best beverage; it seems most of us do not drink enough water daily.

6. Durians and brandy do not mix. Because both are, if one is taken, the other should be avoided.

7. Taking some (fairly) hot Chinese tea after an oily meal will remove that sticky feeling in the throat. Chinese tea is also a good alternative for some drink that causes too much diarrhoea too often.

8. In this country, it is better to drink boiled water; or water from a sealed plastic bottle would be better still. (This raises the question of ice, doesn't it?)

9. Taking more vitamins than the body needs will not do any good, since the excess vitamins will be drained away when we sit on the round thing in the square room.

10. If a fish bone gets stuck in the throat, take, without chewing, lumps of rice or banana. Repeat a few times. If things do not improve, well, the Thai word for 'hospital' is *'rongphaya bahn'*.

11. Nuts (edible types) are very rich in protein. Eat them! Some nuts in the jungle - be careful when trekking -are poisonous while other types may be a waste of time.

12. Vegetables, when fried, lose a good deal of their nutrition. We should eat fresh greens as much and as often as possible, after thoroughly washing them. Many vegetables contain:

Vitamin A	-essential for vision in poor light.
Vitamin B complex	-responsible for growth.
Vitamin C	-lack of which causes scurvy.
Vitamin E.	-used for treating fertility, muscle abnormalities, liver, brain and red blood cells.
Vitamin K	-prevention of hemorrhage, promotion of blood clotting.

13. Grandma also said that too much monosodium gluta mate will make one go bald more quickly.

14. Grandpa said eating chicken feet will help a runner run faster; grandma said they will make hand-writing look like 'fowl scratching'.

15. Grandma said one should always leave the last bit of rice behind on the plate to show we are not selfish and to remember there are those who have no rice to eat. Grandma's grandma said if we leave grains of rice all over the plate, table or floor, our future mate (if we are not married) will have pimples all over the face.

16. A Reader's Digest Encyclopedia says the four basic taste sensations - sweet, sour, bitter and salt are detected in different regions of the tongue: sweetness and saltiness are best appreciated at the tip of the tongue, bitterness at the rear and sourness at the sides.

THE HAWKER OF YESTERDAY

(Note: The following review is not academic research. It is remembered by the older generations whose parents and parents' parents had been or seen hawking as described below.)

The first 'hawking around' must have arisen out of too much left over after a festive dinner, or somebody got bored looking at other members of the household and wanted to take a stroll. Then, probably, the son-in-law could have told the old lady to do something useful instead of just swaggling about.

So..., she could have merely taken a few items in her two hands and hopped over to the nearest neighbour (probably because she wanted to gossip about the no-good son-in-law) and well, she 'sold' whatever she had!

There could be other angles. It could be that some farmer had, say, too much of a produce and in order to get rid of it instead of letting it rot, he took whatever it was and went round hawking!

Another angle could have been generated by a buyer instead of a seller and the seller, after tasting his fortune, began to sell to others as well. Others followed his example and crafty means were devised to move about.

But... whatever it was, we all know that trading began when men wanted to exchange goods, like so long long ago, when cowrie shells were used. And in most parts of all countries, all kinds of mobilisation were utilised: walking, pushing a wheel-barrow or pulling a cart, carrying it on the head, slinging it on the shoulder or back, or using some animals.

In Thailand, we shall go back to just after World War II, some 50 years ago, when almost everybody was poor.

The popular methods of conveying goods were firstly, merely carrying two ratten baskets by hand. Then putting a stick across these two bundles to stride across the shoulder.

Bicycles were the cheapest easy mode of transportation in the '50s; so, because also of narrow tracks people simply rode on these machines and used old car-horns or buffalo bells to announce their presence.

While some merely shouted others shrieked in melodious tones and the smarter ones used hollow bamboo sticks and went 'tok! tok! tok!'

Today, they use electrical equipment: pre-taped casettes, loudspeakers or megaphones and cruising in a pick up.

What did they possibly sell? (apart from them other-in-law's whatever that she sold).

Anything and everything, initially, but insisted some old ladies, eatables, not utilities: food, snacks, drinks, all home made.

Why? Because practically everybody else would have a pail or a plate or a glass at home already. This seems logical.

Will the simple, individual hawker last? Or will he pass away like in advanced countries because of affluence, government control and changing attitudes?

In Thailand the hawker will probably last simply because some kinds of food are not found in restaurants or do-it-yourself packets in supermarkets. Or if they are, it is not the same.

Most hawking food cannot last overnight and the ingredients that go with the food are too much and too troublesome for a big restaurant or superstore to offer profitably. Besides, many locals will say that such duplicates are not 'aroy' to the tongue.

What will increasingly happen is the switch to permanent and stationary sites in front of eating shops as side walks become atrociously overcrowded.

TO YOU ESPECIALLY...

If you have derived something you like from this book - and we hope you have - please pass it on to a friend, or recommend him/her buy a copy.

Thank you for buying this Book, and the Food.

Thai Hawker Food
Win Tun 91

WRAPPING FOOD THAI STYLE

STICKY RICE WITH DIFFERENT TOPPINGS
Khao Niew Moon

◀ **FERMENTED RICE IN COCONUT LEAVES**

▲
STEAMED BANANA CAKES IN LEAVES
Khanom Kluay

PALM CAKE
Khanom Tarn

ROASTED STICKY RICE IN BANANA LEAVES
Khao Niew Ping

ROASTED COCONUT PUDDING IN COCONUT LEAVES

THAI HAWKER FOOD

GLUTINOUS RICE WRAPPED
IN CHINESE PALM LEAVES
Bah Jang

STEAMED STICKY RICE IN BANANA LEAVES
Khao Tom Mud

STEAMED STICKY RICE
IN BANANA LEAVES
Khao Tom Mud Tai

SUGAR-CANES
PEELED AND CUT INTO DISKS

PALM SUGAR IN DRIED
SUGER CANE LEAVES

STEAMED STICKY RICE
IN COCONUT LEAVES

PALM SUGAR
IN BANANA HUSK

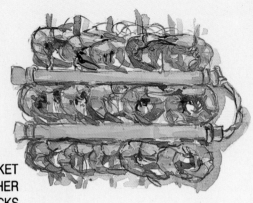

DRIED SHRIMPS FROM PHUKET
PIERCED TOGETHER
BY SHARPENED BAMBOO STICKS

SUN DRIED FISH

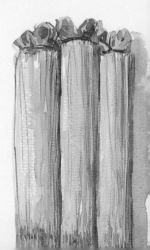

GLUTINOUS RICE
IN BAMBOO

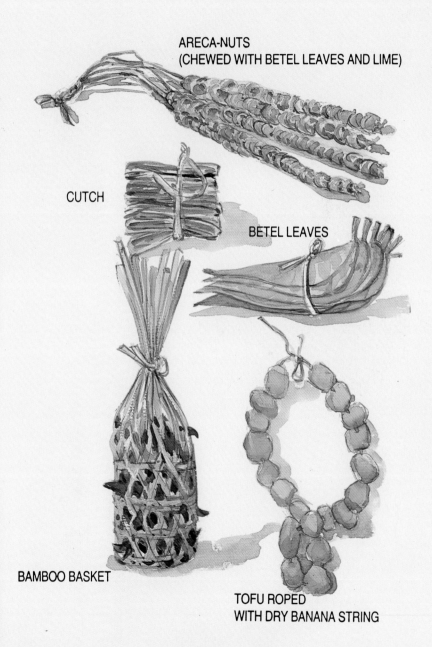

ARECA-NUTS
(CHEWED WITH BETEL LEAVES AND LIME)

CUTCH

BETEL LEAVES

BAMBOO BASKET

TOFU ROPED
WITH DRY BANANA STRING